Facilitating Change in Mental Health

Facilitating Change in Mental Health

Bill Lemmer
Staff Development Department, Nightingale School of Nursing, West Lambeth Health Authority, London

and

Martin Smits
Assistant Chief Nursing Officer, Brighton Health Authority

London
CHAPMAN AND HALL

First published in 1989 by
Chapman and Hall Ltd
11 New Fetter Lane, London EC4P 4EE

Typeset in 10pt Bembo by Best-set Typesetter Ltd
Printed in Great Britain by St Edmundsbury Press Ltd
Bury St Edmunds, Suffolk

ISBN 0 412 33010 5

British Library Cataloguing in Publication Data

Lemmer, Bill, 1942–
Facilitating change in mental health.
1. Great Britain. Mental health services.
Management
I. Title II. Smits, Martin
362.2′068

ISBN 0 412 33010 5

Contents

Acknowledgements

We wish to thank the following people, a number of whom have moved on, for their support and guidance. Janice Cackett, Chief Nursing Officer, West Lambeth Health Authority; Ursula Cowell, Director of Nurse Education, the Nightingale School; Jane Easterbrook, Assistant Director of Nurse Education (Head of Staff Development Dept.); Dennis D'Cruz, Senior Tutor (Psychiatry); Sheila Fowley, Director of Nursing Services; Michael Squizzoni, Assistant Director of Nursing Services; Kathleen McClafferty, Nursing Officer; Joe Gomez, Nursing Officer Personnel; Members of the Nursing Officer Group at Tooting Bec Hospital, staff and patients who participated in the Management of Change Project; Liz Carter, District Nursing Process Co-ordinator; Geoff Haines, Staff Development Tutor; Teachers and librarians at the Education Centre; David Lewin and Judith Lathlean, Nursing Educational Research Unit, Chelsea College (University of London); Pam Smith, Research Tutor, Middlesex Hospital; Alison Kitson, Standards of Care Co-ordinator, Royal College of Nursing; and last but by no means least, John Heatley, Angie Wynne, and Sarah Smits, who enabled us to experience these four years as an enriching process.

In a long project fraught with difficulties, heartache, soul-searching, and plenty of elbow grease, we are deeply indebted to all these people for applying a wealth of experience and for investing their expert skills. This book is evidence of and a testament to our collaboration as educators, practitioners, managers, and researchers.

Preface

This book is about managing change. There are a number of ways of approaching this subject – and that is why we have written a book rather than a journal article. Each chapter in this book describes a different approach to change, for example, personal change, social change, and organizational change. And if one thinks about change in an educational way, and considers how staff develop in a climate of sudden and continuing change, then there is a real need for clear thinking based on practical experience. To this end, we have provided a research base to monitor, evaluate, and direct our work with change.

Today there is an increasing emphasis upon client participation in the planning and delivery of care, upon valuing people who use mental health services in such a way as to empower them to make decisions. These values require new methods of assessment in health and social services work. The changes in emphasis also require new attitudes to enable the various professions, e.g. nursing, medicine, psychology, social work, and occupational therapy, to engage in multi- and inter-disciplinary collaboration.

The traditional attitude to care in mental hospitals, both in the UK and worldwide, has been one of stigmatizing custody, where daily tasks, such as feeding and medication, become more important than individual needs, such as privacy and personal identity. Historical approaches to care are being superseded in favour of closing large psychiatric hospitals and starting afresh with a mental health service in the community. Change is constant; social, economic and political changes affect organizations and individuals, and can be seen at the national and local levels and the personal level.

As they mature and develop people change inside, and change

occurs outside individuals in their environment – whether that is a working environment or one in which they use mental health services. Is change managed? How can it be managed? Do individuals concentrate on their personal views of the here-and-now? Should the focus be on the transition between closing hospitals and starting replacement services? Does one look forward and act upon predicted needs, such as increasing consumer involvement in mental health care and prevention? The agendas for change are many, and in this book we hope to provide a number of stimulating ideas and reveal a wide range of strategies that are coordinated by the local steering group.

As a staff development tutor and researcher, we are interested in finding ways to prepare people for change, and the ways in which change is introduced and the process whereby participants gain self-sufficiency in new standards of care are themes in this book. In particular, we explore methods of facilitating change as part of training; however, how change is sustained, or whether it is to be permanent, are moot points, as far as we are concerned, because change is a continuous and complex dynamic of life – not a static entity, but part of what is inside people and what is outside them. It is consistent both with the values of adult education and the new mental health services that the authority in and responsibility for change must ultimately (to be lasting, in so far as further change is possible) rest with the people who use our services, whether they are staff who are our clients or members of the public who need mental health care.

A word on how to use this book. In the introduction we explain the Management of Change Project, and each chapter illustrates a feature of this project, for example, research, education, organizational change, and the values of psychiatric nursing. Using the project as a case in point, the chapters raise broad questions concerning change in the mental health field. Here no attempt is made either to generalize from our work or to lay claim to universal truths as a result of it; we are sharing and disseminating three years of work in a context which explores the rationale behind its processes. The book describes the development of a continuing educational project, and concludes by recommending a model for change that is based upon the real and practical events which we observed and recorded.

In this book we refer to people according to their roles during the project, although today many have new jobs. Following the project, the hospital was completely reorganized, and two of its products – the Nursing Development Team and the Model Wards Training Project – were abandoned. We continue to use the language common at the time of our work, such as 'psychogeriatric' and 'patients', whereas today words such as 'elderly care' and 'residents' are commonplace.

Bill Lemmer
Martin Smits

Introduction

In 1983 Bill Lemmer was appointed Nursing Officer, Inservice Training, for the nursing assistants of a large Victorian psychiatric institution. The chain of events begun by that appointment has resulted, six years later, in the publication of this book.

Throughout the text there are references to the work of those years, and in Chapter 6 we present that work as a case study. The book, as a whole, is about facilitating change in general, not the reporting of a specific project. We feel that the illustrations from a real-life example of change in practice greatly enhance the work, and we hope that they also add credibility to our writing, demonstrating that we are not just theorizing about change, but do have first-hand experience of it! From whatever background you come, we hope that the many illustrations help to enrich your understanding of the business of facilitating change. To put the illustrations into context we outline here the background to our work and the settings and timings of events.

Project. Our work with change began initially with a responsibility for the training of nursing assistants, unqualified nurses. Eventually it involved all the staff who came into contact with this group of nurses and became known as the Management of Change Project.

Aim. Inevitably as the project grew the aims developed and changed. In outline, the essence of the project was to:

1. describe and evaluate attitudes to patient care among nursing assistants and qualified staff
2. use that information as a basis for future change

3. measure the change that takes place as a result of various educational inputs.

We moved from evaluation of a school-based training for nursing assistants to an evaluation of a ward-based educational programme for all staff.

Location. The project concerned the staff of Tooting Bec Hospital in south London.

Management. At the start of the work Tooting Bec Hospital was part of the St Thomas's Hospital (Teaching) District although this became known as West Lambeth Health Authority. The hospital itself lies in the geographical boundaries of Wandsworth Health Authority although there are no management ties with that authority.

The building and site. The fabric of the hospital reflects its Victorian origins. Located in spacious green grounds, it occupies a site adjacent to common land that stretches in an interrupted belt across south London. Development has long since leap-frogged this green belt and the hospital is now found in an increasingly fashionable suburb of London. The health authority is well aware of the site's increasing value.

The buildings themselves are of brick, organized in blocks of three floors around a central administrative block. Behind its iron railings and high walls the hospital looks the picture of institutional containment. Although familiarity has probably bred contempt in much of the local population, the caged cat-walks still strike a note of fear in many. In historical terms it is a place of note, earning its Victorian title of the Surrey Lunatic Asylum.

People involved. When it opened in 1903, the hospital had 27 wards. By 1926 this had grown to 67 wards with 2400 patients. By the start of the project there were in the region of 900 patients. Initially the project was concerned with the 130 nursing assistants in 40 areas. As the project developed five wards became the focus and these had a total of 103 patients with 78 nursing staff (some part-time), approximately half (53%) of the staff being unqualified nurses.

The wards. The wards involved in the project were 'classified' as psychogeriatric, and although today they would be referred to as wards for the elderly mentally ill, we have used throughout this book the language of the actual setting. Although much had been done to disguise the institutional nature of the internal aspects of the building, nothing could really hide the true nature of the place. High ceilings, large rooms, big windows, and antiquated services (e.g. kitchen facilities) typified the wards. In general, the furnishings reflected the institutional nature of the hospital, with old iron beds, plastic chairs and large cast-iron baths.

Chronology. The sequence and timing of the major events of the project are listed below. Throughout the book we refer to specific parts of our work as illustrations in the discussion, and the reader may use this list for reference purposes.

Date	*Educational input*	*Evaluative technique*
1983	formal one- and two-week, school-based training for nursing assistants	participant/non-participant observation + unstructured interviews
1984	new training course for nursing assistants	semi-structured interviews
1985	facilitated ward-based educational groups	pre- and post-questionnaires + diaries
1986	ward sister's group	therapeutic nursing function indicator +
	ward-based Quality Circles	diaries circle notes

We refer to each of the above years as phases of the project.

Key components. We argue in this book that there are several *key components* in any work with change and we present them here, so that they do not take readers by surprise in the text (explanatory details are found in the text).

Groupwork as an educational process;
Research approach to social investigation, particularly the cyclical approach known as 'action research';

Education;
Management.

Combined together, these components are a means of taking action.

You will find that the key issues for the Management of Change Project were the individuality of care, the continuity of care, and the responsibility for care. At the beginning of Chapter 9 the reader will find a summary of the book and of each chapter.

Armed with this introduction, we invite you to read on, browsing through the pages and picking out that which is of particular interest to you, and hope that our exploration is worthwhile, informative, and rewarding.

— 1 —
Values in psychiatric nursing

1.1 A BRIEF HISTORICAL PERSPECTIVE

Retrospective views can be difficult because each time you look back it looks different! From this point of view, then, each historical visit is enriched, or not, in the light of current experience, knowledge, and culture. The look-back in this section is influenced by the question: what part has mental hospital care in Britain played in the development of psychiatric nursing values?

By 1900 psychiatry was influenced by organic theories of disease. This influence probably dates from the time of William Harvey's (1628) paper, *'De motu cordis'*, where he claimed to discover blood circulating in the body. This inside-out view of disorder can be illustrated (see Fig. 1.1) by contrasting the reductionist position of the natural sciences with the holistic position of the social sciences.

The medical practitioner's assumptions about mental disorder was underscored by a Victorian attitude that it was worse than disease; it was bad. And the people who were seen to be disordered were dangerous.

Amid these prevailing views at the turn of the century, early-nineteenth-century reformers wished to free lunatics from the inhumane practices of the workhouse. They intended to transfer some of the pauper patients to small institutions. These places, having a more informal regime than that of the workhouse, would by appropriate for humane and personalised care. William Tuke, a Quaker tea-merchant, founded in 1793 the Retreat at York. At this hospital for the mentally ill he introduced the notion of care that was centred upon the individual. Such care was to be based upon

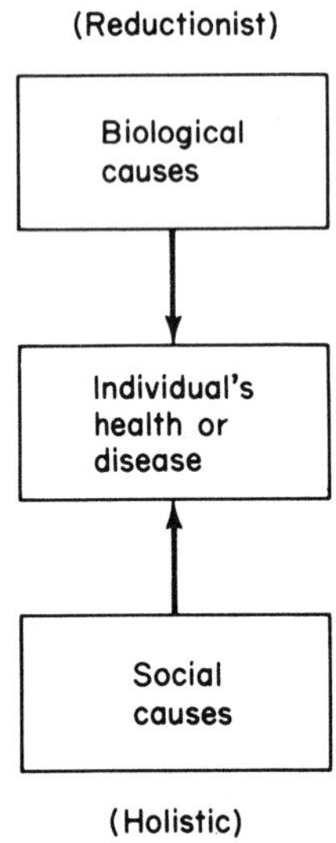

Fig. 1.1 The individual is viewed as being at meeting-point of biological or internal causes, and of social or external causes. The diagram contrasts types of explanation of the phenomena of health and disease, from a natural sciences and social sciences perspective (from Walker and Wright, 1985, Bk 1, p. 82).

kindness, tolerance, and minimum restraint. Tuke's initiative coincided, in 1793, with the unbonding of lunatics by a French physician, Philippe Pinel, at the Bicêtre in Paris.

A physician by the name of John Bucknill wrote in 1853 that Pinel 'vindicated the rights of science against the usurpations of superstition and brutality and rescued the victims of mental disease from the exorcist and the gaoler'.

John Conolly, whose medical thesis, in 1821, was on insanity and melancholia, introduced the notion of individualized care at Hanwell Asylum, near London. Criteria for determining activity for patients was that the patients should be interested in it. This initiative to give credence to patients' values was coupled with a commitment to abolish restraints where possible, e.g. strait-waistcoats, hand-straps, and leg-locks.

Tuke's grandson, Samuel, wrote in 1813 that the quality of care is achieved by 'limiting the power of the attendant, making it in his interest to obtain the good opinion of those under his care'. Physical security, he said, militated against the exercise of proper nursing practice (Parker, 1985). In other words, the emergent role of the nurse might be about how a relationship could be used to help a person in distress.

However, a biological view of health and illness (Fig. 1.1), along with social attitudes and political influences, were to be the values upon which mental health care would be organized. Despite some significant, isolated reforms, the emphasis upon controlling emotions and treating people in batches resulted in a mental health service provision dependent upon drugs, namely potassium bromide, chloral hydrate, paraldehyde, barbiturates, such as Veronal, and finally the neuroleptics, such as Largactil. The asylums, first considered to be places of safety, became remote dumping grounds for unwanted citizens. There were no plausible explanations for what was viewed as lunatic behaviour, nor was there any effective treatment for mental disorder. By the twentieth century hospitals were accommodating an 'increasing tide of chronic pauper patients':

> The personal quality of the care and the family atmosphere of the 1830s and 1840s gave place to a restrictive and coercive regime. The patients and the small staff of attendants were locked away from the world behind high walls, barred windows and a morbid culture borne of prejudice, fear, and isolation. (Roth and Bluglass, 1985, p.229)

Psychiatric nursing did not exist at this time. The first course for attendants was established in 1890 by the Royal Medico-Psychological Association (RMPA, now the Royal College of Psychiatrists). The General Nursing Council (GNC) formed a register, part of which was for mental nurses, in 1919. But the RMPA training was preferred by employers until 1951 when the GNC, controlled by and run for general nurses from its inception, took full responsibility (Brooking, 1984). Therefore, the values of mental nursing were tied to those which employers placed upon the kind of service provision they intended.

Florence Nightingale was clearly not training nurses to become skilled attendants. However, a number of registered nurses saw the mental hospitals as providing a good opportunity to gain quick promotion as asylum matrons. Attendants were treated like domestic servants, with comparable wages. By the turn of the century they lived on the wards and were, like the patients, strictly disciplined. Many of the attendants were used to supervise working parties of patient labour.

Female staff worked on one side of the mental hospital and male attendants on the other. The women's side was associated with general nursing and vocational values, along with a higher social background than that on the male side. The men tended to reject nursing professionalism, such as it was, and the medical model of nursing; the ascendancy of unionization in mental hospitals was a rapid by-product of this interesting split in the values of health care providers (Brooking, 1984).

The large asylums, traditionally the exclusive responsibility of public authorities, continued to lead to impersonal custodial regimes, lack of privacy, and lack of social and intellectual stimuli. The staff became as institutionalized as the patients.

The sheer number and weight of these significant historical factors which we have discussed have combined strongly such that it is not surprising that the values of the past are transferred to the present day. Among these factors are the social class of most of the Victorian patients, the prevailing moral attitudes, the kinds of explanation for mental health and disease, the hospital culture itself, and the development of general nursing. A picture emerges, then, of how the past has influenced contemporary psychiatric nursing. The crucial part played by mental hospital care in the development of nursing is that the values of the past have been transferred to the present.

1.2 CLASSIC NOTIONS ON CAUSE AND EFFECT IN LONG-TERM CARE

Given this historical perspective, how might we think about *facilitating change* by considering influential causes and effects of long-term care?

Notions of persistence and lack of change are basic to the definition of the long-stay, chronic, or institutionalized person. The major issue in any definition, according to Craig and Hyatt (1978), is individual autonomy and independence vs family 'belonging' and emotional dependency. If you were to draw a line straight across the middle box in Fig. 1.1 (i.e across an individual's health or disease) and call it, for instance, a continuum of life/equilibrium, you would probably expect to see growth and personal maturity, from emotional dependency within a family toward individual autonomy and independence (Fig. 1.2).

Dependence ________________________________ Independence

(continuum of life and equilibrium)

Fig. 1.2 An individual's health or disease.

The most relevant feature in this process may be how a lack of control produced helplessness – lack of control would reduce motivation to effect change and inhibit the ability to learn that responses can control outcomes. For example, a skilled nursing response by a particular individual would be different to the same individual's reaction at home. The point here is that a normal loss of equilibrium (from independence to dependence), such as the death of a spouse, could be made worse by a hospital that fosters emotional and physical dependency.

Barton (1959) considers a dead environment as an illness added to an illness in the way people who are patients are treated. This creates 'mental bed sores', which are a function of the way staff operate in the same custodial and impersonal way, day after day in an unchanging, unstimulating environment. The effects of this persistent lack of change include an increase in dependency.

Yoder (1977) and Ackerman (1958) refer to alienation as a central notion in mental health care. They see alienation as 'prolonged adolescence'. Crowcroft (1967) refers to the custodial environment as a contributing factor in causing the regression which he sees as mental illness – the return to early stages of development. Again using the model in Fig. 1.2, the effects of becoming alienated, while losing equilibrium along the continuum, are despair, powerlessness, and hopelessness.

Thus the central feature of this vicious circle of causes and effects in long-term care is the lack of positive change and the increasing downward spiral to dependency. Laing (1967) suggests that there are physical developments undermining this process in so far as the biochemistry of an individual is highly sensitive to social circumstance. Furthermore, Vernon (1971) concludes that normal perception can be maintained only in a constantly changing environment. The power to attend is only partially under voluntary control. Under certain conditions one cannot, as an observer, deliberately maintain one's attention for an indefinite period. Vernon argues that a deadening, unchanging environment produces an inhibitory emotional effect which is aroused before complete perception occurs. This means that, as time passes, routine, ritual, and a lack of stimulation combine to prevent the recognition of a newly introduced object, person, or event. In other words, not only does nothing perceptually change, but change is not perceived. The effect of no change further disrupts unconscious, automatic, biological processes that are essential for attention and discrimination.

These causes and effects reside, as it were, inside the historical values discussed in the first section of this chapter. Therefore, what is transferred from the past to the present is not just the values *per se*, but real environmental and personal problems in transacting the business of nursing; thus the tension between innovation and routine, between discovery and management, and between the values of a process or client-centred approach to care and a product or task-centred approach.

Menzies's (1960) classic enquiry identifies several features which, by her study, would typify nursing organization and nursing behavior:

1. The splitting of nurse–patient relationships (by giving nurses a few tasks to perform upon a large number of patients);
2. Ritualistic task performance (this refers to the task-oriented approach, with little variation or individual interpretation in relation to a patient's needs; therefore, the blocking effect upon nurse–patient relationships is reinforced);
3. Denial of feelings – i.e. nurses being 'taught' not to get close to or be involved with patients;
4. Depersonalization of nurse and patient (perceived by Nichols, (1984), as nurses being taught the attitude that they are interchangeable with one another).

This tendency to depersonalize is also noted by Stockwell (1972) and Towell (1975). Menzies, Stockwell, and Towell demonstrate the effects upon nurses and patients of the absence of interpersonal relationships.

Moreover, Altschul (1981) argues that we, as health care providers, are causes of dependency effects in patients. Once we call sufferers 'patients', she reasons, they soon adopt a sick role that is every bit as passive as the former inmate role, described by Goffman (1961) in *Asylums*. Altschul writes that this sick role:

> confers on the 'patient' the right to self-indulgence...to expect medical treatment. It absolves him...of responsibility for his behaviour...it deprives him of the power to make decisions about his own care...in determining his own life pattern.

If the sick role absolves a person from responsibility for his/her illness, and this implies that the person is no longer the agency determining changes that occur, then the person who performs this function would engineer passivity in the sick person (Baruch and Treacher, 1978). On the other hand, the causes and effects of entering the sick role, that is, the process of becoming mentally ill, are complicated by our ability as individuals to use 'madness' to control and influence close relatives and mental health workers (Scott, 1973; Mechanic, 1969).

The cyclical and damaging nature of these classic notions about the causes and effects of long-term care are a reflection of the mental hospital system. It is a closed system that denies the patients as a peer group. Traditionally the mental hospital has been service-centred and has failed to supply the human needs of self-respect, self-esteem, and self-identity. The values of nursing and the causes and effects of long-term care have been tied together in this tradition in such a way that change has been fraught with problems.

1.3 ATTEMPTS TO CHANGE NURSING

Tom Main, referring to nurses' therapeutic engagement with patients, writes:

> The nurses had owned painful distresses, concealed ailments connected with certain patients' ailments, and by disclosing these. . .they arrived not only at an increased capacity to recognise uncertainties. . .but a personal easement in it. They became less afraid of difficult situations and surer at their craft. (Main, 1968, p. 41)

Main refers to nursing in a therapeutic community, the Cassel Hospital. Here change is a feature of the nurses' and patients' individual lives as an instrumental focus of treatment. Because change is also evident in the structure of the therapeutic community, attempts to change nursing elsewhere have been modelled upon it.

David Towell (1975) found, as have others before him, that patient improvement is not only consequent on particular medical treatments. It is also a function of the individual's immediate interpersonal relations and of group and institutional processes that characterize the mental hospital in which he/she is living. Attempting to effect therapeutic change within institutionalized settings generates role conflict and tensions 'created by open communication'. In effect, the hospital becomes the patient. Towell compared nurses' work on a traditional ward with the nursing on a ward in which the lines of communication were increased. He reports that nurses' perceptions on the ward designated for effecting therapeutic change in patients was notably different in the nurses' focus upon patients' individual problems.

Peplau (1952), who devised a model for psychiatric nursing, supports the view that therapeutic change and communication cannot be about custodial activities. Nursing is not about restraint, protection, cleanliness, or order. Instead she stresses therapeutic use of the self as a focus for interpersonal techniques that enables patients to experience personality growth and maturity. This, she says, is how people who are patients get better: the nurse uses his/her personality as the main tool in nursing – nurses, by examining their relationship with patients, can enable the latter to develop their own values and regain the equilibrium referred to in Fig. 1.2. (While this is an oversimplification of Peplau, it is not our task here to consider the strengths and weaknesses of this model.)

Regardless of the intentions of nurses to make changes, the environment or social context of nursing will no doubt impinge upon the quality of care. Altschul (1972), for example, has established several factors which prevail in hospitals; these factors affect the interaction between nurses and patients and make their relationships dependent upon aspects of hospital life. They include the availability of beds; a consultant's name; a policy of moving patients from ward to ward as they improve or relapse; the size of a ward and the size of the hospital; staff–patient ratio and expenditure; hospital organization and the physical condition of the place; treatment ideologies; and staff attitudes. Altschul has identified one of the specific contributions of in-patient nursing, as compared with treatment in the community, that is the effect that living in the ward is intended to have on the therapeutic outcome of a patient's day. She argues that this outcome depends upon the extent to which the patient is enabled later on to form new relationships as a result of his/her relations with the staff.

Stanton and Schwartz (1954), and Caudill (1958), also view the psychiatric hospital as a negative or unhealthy social system. They found that the quality of behaviour in all areas of hospital life is affected. The institutional regime had a set of properties in it which caused the system to be socially unfit.

Jones (1979) suggests nurses should change – and that they could change the social system of the hospital. He maintains they could achieve this if they pursue the principles of two-way communication of content and feelings, information-sharing, listening, interacting, and of discussing with a view to learning and growth. Towell (1975) has found this is not entirely realistic in an institution with two different treatment ideologies, namely with one ward having a traditional ethos which is unchallenged, and another with a therapeutic emphasis upon change towards individualized care. Nurses in such an institution have 'concerns' in both settings and also have to come to terms with 'social therapy'. The examples of attempts to change nursing indicate that change needs to run right through the organization, as well as focusing intervention in a particular area of the organization.

Previous attempts to make changes have defined the conflicts between innovation and traditional psychiatric nursing, between the rights of patients and nurses and demands of institutional life, between professional nursing and custodial care, and between caring relationships and the hospital as a social system.

1.4 THE SEARCH FOR A KNOWLEDGE BASE

Current practice in mental health care and psychiatric nursing is eclectic: it is based upon what appears to be best from various doctrines, methods, or styles of helping people. Theories that Beck and others (1984) perceive to be borrowed and used in nursing occur in the work of: Freud (1914), Sullivan (1953), Adolph Meyer (1957), George Mead (1934), Emil Kraepelin (1904), Margaret Mead (1928), Erik Erikson (1965), Skinner (1953), Maslow (1970), and Piaget (1952).

Nurses have yet to adopt a central paradigm upon which to base their practice. Instead we pick and choose from here and there, using a wide variety of criteria; but perhaps most frequently we use professional judgement coupled with an intimate knowledge of the environment and the client. Perhaps the main problems with borrowing theories is the assumptions that are borrowed with them; and aligned to this, we appear to have no agreed framework in which borrowing takes place. Our practice is based upon the theoretical notions we hold dear, but how do we derive these notions?

How do we share them in a way in which practice can be consistent? How is knowledge used?

Individuals' self-concept is related to their level of functioning. This is a well-documented focus in caring for people who are personally distressed (Jasinski, 1985). The current state of the art in psychiatric nursing stresses skills in communication, interpersonal relationships, and personal growth (Altschul, 1972, 1985; Peplau, 1952, 1957, 1960, 1962, 1968, 1978; Bunch, 1985; Burnard, 1986). Implicit here is not only the borrowing of concepts, but their formulating anew, the practical application of ideas, with a high value placed on learning and change. The promotion of self-esteem is considered a professional as well as an applied essential that is a requisite of nursing practice.

Early nursing research frequently uses methods from other disciplines. These include constructs and relationships developed in laboratory settings. Naturally these are not easily transferred to the practice of psychiatric nursing. Given this reliance on other disciplines, it is not surprising that developing a theory unique to nursing has been slow. Moreover, it could be argued that this is back-to-front anyhow; i.e. perhaps the development of a knowledge base would best be done at the interface between nurses and their clients (Dickoff and James, 1968; Glaser and Strauss, 1967)? From this latter viewpoint, we can further process Fig. 1.1 into a new construct (Fig. 1.3).

Most of nursing's theoretical models are based upon systems theory; in terms of Fig. 1.3, they are top–down models. The belief that to be scientific you must also be systematic is open to scrutiny, to say the least. It is claimed that nursing is about problem-solving and is therefore scientific. The sciences which nurses have borrowed from determine their approach to making assertions about what nursing *is*. From the bottom–up viewpoint, it might be argued that, considering the client's values especially, the nursing models do not provide a practical framework for borrowing, thus the knowledge borrowed cannot be used to the client's advantage. Diers (1979), McFarlane (1980), and Chenitz and Swanson (1984) indicate that the models of King (1981), Rogers (1970), and Roy (1976) may be inconsistent with the investigative values and humanistic philosophy of nursing practice. The notion of deciding upon a person's mental health care by using nursing values – never mind applying them systematically to targeted problems – may prejudice an individual's assessment.

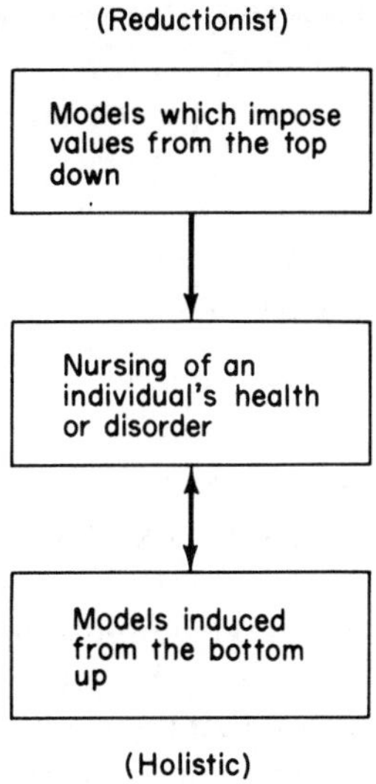

Fig. 1.3 A construct for deriving useful knowledge.

Interestingly, Johnston and others (1982) have looked at the same four nursing models, and found them not necessarily consistent with the borrowed theory which is used by psychiatric nurses, for example, Sullivan's. Peplau (1952) draws heavily upon the work of Sullivan; and much of psychiatric nursing is based upon the importance of interpersonal aspects of nurse–client relationships. The nurse, then, uses his/her personality as a principal instrument in promoting mental health care. The inconsistency lies in the intended use of what is borrowed, i.e. between the product-oriented structure of problem-solving and the essential autonomy of individual nurses to be free to develop helping relationships. The way in which relationships are made, to foster the personal growth and maturity of the client, may not follow an established pattern or system because all things are not equal. Relationship-building is not academic in a context where reality is, to some extent, distorted. This difference in the way in which nurses make relationships for helping is particularly evident outside hospital and in the community.

The way in which nursing practices have been transferred from the past to the present is in fact similar to the way in which we appear to derive knowledge, as the similarities between Figs 1.1

and 1.3 indicate. It would appear that psychiatric nursing needs to attempt to change the way it derives and uses knowledge at the same time as attempting to make practical changes, as we have seen in the problematic attempts to innovate therapeutic community nursing in hospitals. A model for change which encompasses both knowledge and practice may provide a framework in which clients benefit more than from those values which are alien to them and imposed upon them.

1.5 THE TRANSITION FROM HOSPITAL TO COMMUNITY

The World Health Organisation symposium, in Salzburg, in 1971 found that traditional psychiatric hospitals were located too far away from populated centres, that they had no re-socialization programmes, with no therapeutic contact between staff and patients, and in general created an impression of people being 'put away'. And, in addition, it was impossible to provide adequate staffing in such places. Trimbos (1980) traced the four-centuries-old heritage of using asylums as an instrument at the service of public order and the law. Treatment was an efficient means of social control which, he argues, marks the psychiatric institution of the modern era.

Baert (1980) points to contemporary social and cultural trends with implications for mental health care. These include the decline in family support systems, the individual's growing sense of remoteness from the decision-making process, and the increased personal expectations of a consumer-oriented society with a decreased personal tolerance for stress.

Representatives from the fifteen countries which took part in a European workshop on alternatives to mental hospitals, in Ghent, Belgium, in 1980 found no way for large psychiatric hospitals to be reconciled with caring approaches to psychiatric disorders (Towell, 1980).

Caring for long-term users of mental health services, as well as other users, demands teaching and psychosocial skills that are relatively new to nursing. Nurses are called upon to deal with the meaning that illness has for the client. This variable of clients' perception of what their experience means is likely to determine how they manage their relationships, and the self.

Client participation in the planning of nursing care and involvement in the development of new services is a significant new notion in mental health care. Consumer involvement dramatically alters the nature of nursing care. Goal setting, reviewing progress, anticipating change, all become joint and collaborative exercises. This is a particularly difficult issue for service providers as the formerly rivalrous and competitive disciplines come together for the transition to new mental health services based in the community. It will be particularly difficult for clients in this transition, as they may also be burdened with feelings of isolation, lack of an outlet for emotional expression, and experience loss of control over day-to-day events. To negotiate with professionals over the priorities of care may not be realistic in the uncertainty of new management initiatives which are strictly from the top down.

At the same time, the focus in developing new services is, first, on closure of mental hospitals, and second on the administrative commitment to establish community bases. Scant attention is paid to preparing staff and hospital clients for change unless they have a high enough profile for the new-base criteria. The transition has caused alarm among hospital staff. And the lack of resources in the community for patients coming from hospital has also caused some disquiet and concern on a wider scale (Audit Commission for Local Authorities, 1986).

Perhaps the healthiest sign in the transition from hospital to community is the diversity of planning around community mental health centres, in order to meet needs which are unique to a locale. The transition is leading us, as health care providers and service users and potential users, to think about psychiatric nursing in a different way than we have in the past. This new thinking will need to have clarity and meaning for nurses, clients, and interdisciplinary workers.

REFERENCES

Ackerman, N. (1958) *The Psychodynamics of Family Life*, Basic Books, New York.

Altschul, A.T. (1972) *Patient–Nurse Interaction: a study of interaction patterns in acute psychiatric wards*, Churchill Livingstone, Edinburgh.

Altschul, A.T. (1981) Issues in psychiatric nursing, in L. Hockey, (ed.) *Current Issues in Nursing*, Churchill Livingstone, London.

Altschul, A.T. (ed.) (1985) *Psychiatric Nursing: Recent Advances in Nursing 12*, Churchill Livingstone, London.

Audit Commission for Local Authorities in England and Wales. (1986) *Making a Reality of Community Care*, HMSO, London.

Baert, A.E. (1980) Why do we need alternatives? *World Hospitals* **16**(4), 19–20.

Barton, R. (1959) *Institutional Neurosis*. John Wright and Sons, London.

Baruch, G. and Treacher, A. (1978) *Psychiatry Observed*, Routledge and Kegan Paul, London.

Beck, C.M., Rawlins, R.P. and Williams, S.R. (eds) (1984) *Mental Health – Psychiatric Nursing: a holistic life-cycle approach*, C.V. Mosby Co., St Louis, MO.

Brooking, J.I. (1984) *Advanced Psychiatric Nursing Education in Britain*, University of London, London.

Bucknill, J. (ed.) (1853) *The Asylum Journal*, **1**, 1, November 15 (reprinted in *The Asylum Journal of Mental Science*, 1855).

Bunch, E.H. (1985) Therapeutic communication: is it possible for psychiatric nurses to engage in this on an acute psychiatric ward?, in A.T. Altschul, (ed.) *Psychiatric Nursing*, Ch 3, pp. 43–62.

Burnard, P. (1986) Picking up the pieces. *Nursing Times*, **28**(17), 37–39.

Caudill, W. (1958) *The Psychiatric Hospital as a Small Society*, Harvard University Press, Cambridge, MA.

Chenitz, W.C. and Swanson, J.M. (1984) Surfacing nursing process: a method for generating nursing theory from practice, *J. Adv. Nursing*, **9**, 205–15.

Craig, A.E. and Hyatt, B.A. (1978) Chronicity in mental illness: a theory on the role of change. *Perspectives in Psychiatric Care*, **3**(16); 139–54.

Crowcroft, A. (1967) *The Psychotic: understanding madness*. Penguin Books Ltd, Harmondsworth.

Dickoff, J. and James, P. (1968) A theory of theories. *Nursing Research*, **17**(3), 197–203.

Diers, D. (1979) *Research in Nursing Practice*, J.B. Lippincott, Philadelphia.

Erikson, E. (1965) *Childhood and Society*, Hogarth Press, London.

Freud, S. (1914) Totem and Taboo, in J. Strachey (ed.) standard edition of *The complete psychological works of Sigmund Freud*, Vol. 13. The Hogarth Press London.

Glaser, B. and Strauss, A. (1967) *The Discovery of Grounded Theory: strategies for qualitative research*, Aldine Press, Chicago.

Goffman, E. (1961) *Asylums*, Penguin Books Ltd, Harmondsworth.

Jasinski, J. (1985) Community adaptation: a correlate of the self concept for the chronic psychiatric patient, in A.T. Altschul (ed.) *Psychiatric Nursing: recent advances in nursing 12*, Ch 4, Churchill Livingstone, London, pp. 63–84.

Johnston, R.L. and Fitzpatrick, J.J. (1982) Relevance of psychiatric mental health nursing theories to nursing models, in J. Fitzpatrick, A. Whall, R.L. Johnston, J. Floyd, (eds) *Nursing Models and Their Psychiatric Mental Health Applications*, Ch 1, Robert J. Brady Co, Bowie, Maryland, pp. 1–16.

Jones, M. (1979) Preface, in R.D. Hinshelwood and N. Manning, (eds) *Therapeutic Communities: reflections and progress*, Routledge and Kegan Paul, London.

King, I.M. (1981) *A Theory for Nursing: Systems, Concepts, Process*, John Wiley and Sons Inc., New York.

Kraepelin, E. (1904) *Vergleichende Psychiatrie Journal*, (*Transcultural Psychiatric Review*) **11**, 108, (1974).

Laing, R.D. (1967) *The Politics of Experience and the Bird of Paradise*. Penguin Books, Harmondsworth.

Main, T. (1968) The Ailment, in E. Barnes, (ed.) *Psychosocial Nursing: studies from the Cassel Hospital*, Tavistock Publications, London.

Maslow, A.H. (1970) *Motivation and Personality* (2nd edn), Harper and Row Publishers Inc., New York.

McFarlane, E.A. (1980) Nursing theory: the comparison of four theoretical proposals. *J. Adv. Nursing*, **5**, 3–19.

Mead, G. (1934) *Mind, Self, and Society*, Chicago University Press, Chicago.

Mead, M. (1928) *Coming of Age in Somoa*. William Morrow and Co., New York.

Mechanic, P. (1969) *Mental Health and Social Policy*, Prentice-Hall Inc., Englewood Cliffs, N.J.

Menzies, I.E.P. (1960) *The Functioning of Social Systems as a Defense Against Anxiety: a report on a study of the nursing service of a general hospital*, Tavistock Publications, London.

Meyer, A. (1957) *Psychobiology: a science of man*, Charles C. Thomas, Springfield, IL.

Nichols, K.A. (1984) *Psychological Care in Physical Illness*, Croom Helm, London.

Orem, D.E. (1980) *Nursing: concepts of practice* (2nd edn), McGraw-Hill, New York.

Parker, E. (1985) The development of secure provision, in L. Gostin (ed.) *Secure Provision: a review of special services for the mentally ill and mentally handicapped in England and Wales*.

Peplau, H.E. (1952) *Interpersonal Relations in Nursing: a conceptual frame of reference for psychodynamic nursing*, G.P. Putnam's Sons, New York.

Peplau, H.E. (1957) Therapeutic concepts. *National League for Nursing: aspects of psychiatric nursing* (26), pp. 1–30.

Peplau, H.E. (1960) Talking with patients. *Am. J. Nursing*, **60**(7), 964–6.

Peplau, H.E. (1962) Interpersonal techniques: the crux of psychiatric nursing. *Am. J. Nursing*, **62**(6), 50–54.
Peplau, H.E. (1968) Psychotherapeutic strategies. *Perspectives in Psychiatric Care*, **6**(6) November/December pp. 264–89.
Peplau, H.E. (1978) Psychiatric nursing: role of nurses and psychiatric nurses. *International Nursing Review*, **25**(2) March/April, pp. 41–7
Piaget, J. (1952) *The Origin of Intelligence in Children*, International Universities Press Inc., New York.
Rogers, M.E. (1970) *An Introduction to the Theoretical Basis of Nursing*, F.A. Davis, Philadelphia.
Roth, M. and Bluglass, R. (1985) A postscript on the discussions at the Cambridge Conference on Society, Psychiatry and the Law, in L. Gostin, (ed.) *Secure Provision*, Tavistock Publications, London.
Roy, C. (1976) *Introduction to Nursing: an adaptation model*, Prentice-Hall Inc., Englewood Cliffs, NJ.
Scott, R.D. (1973) The treatment barrier: Part 1. *Br. J. Medical Psychol.*, **46**, 45.
Skinner, B.F. (1953) *Science and Human Behavior*. The Macmillan Co., New York.
Stanton, A. and Schwartz, M. (1954) *The Mental Hospital*. Basic Books, New York.
Stockwell, F. (1972) *The Unpopular Patient*, Royal College of Nursing, London.
Sullivan, H.S. (1953) *The Interpersonal Theory of Psychiatry*, W.W. Norton and Co. Inc., New York.
Towell, D. (1975) *Understanding Psychiatric Nursing*, Royal College of Nursing, London.
Towell, D. (1980) European workshop on alternatives to mental hospitals: a personal perspective. *World Hospitals*, **16**(4), 17–32.
Trimbos, C. (1980) Developments in intra-mural and extra-mural alternatives to the mental hospital. *World Hospitals* **16**(4), 22–5.
Vernon, M.D. (1971) *The Psychology of Perception*, Penguin Books, Harmondsworth.
Walker, S. and Wright, D. (eds) (1985) *Studying Health and Disease, BK I*, Open University Press, Milton Keynes.
Yoder, S.A. (1977) Alienation as a way of life. *Perspectives in Psychiatric Care*, **15**(2), 66–71.

— 2 —
Educational perspectives

One of our earliest findings in the Management of Change Project (1983–6) was that the nursing assistants (NAs) had difficulty in using what they had learned in a mental hospital setting. What was demonstrated by them in practice during their course was not evident afterwards in their practice setting, even though the skills gained had been apparent during the course in a ward where part of their training took place. What is taught and what is practised are different because of the way in which the custodial culture and hierarchical organization of the hospital permeate the delivery of care. This assumption is explored in the project; and teaching has to embrace all grades of staff in methods of learning which can reveal the truth: how do you know that an educational activity enhances both the carer and the care? In our case, change goes hand in hand with learning. If the culture of the mental hospital seems to prevent or inhibit the outcome of learning being observable in practice, then changes which experiment with teaching, learning, and practice must be tried and tested until a resolution is found. Bearing these points in mind, with what kind of notion does this leave us in terms of education?

In this chapter we address the above questions in three ways. First, we examine four educational perspectives and reflect upon their relevance to the particular problem identified in the NA course evaluations. This is followed by a worked example of how our own community (in West Lambeth) relates to current curriculum planning. Just as the environment in which caring takes place is in transition, from hospital to community bases, from task-centred to patient-centred care, so too is the learning environment in flux. In addition, a measure of the difference between what is on offer educationally and the social reality of the emergent practice setting becomes clear in the analysis of a cultural situation. Concluding our discussion of educational perspectives, we examine the comparison between learning and change. An explanation of how these themes relate to one another gives us some idea of what methods continuing education might use. There may also be indications here of what essential attributes a change agent might possess.

2.1 PERSPECTIVES ON EDUCATION

We outline here four schools of thought, which reflect different educational developments from psychological frameworks to learning theory: (1) behaviourist, (2) psychoanalytic, (3) cognitive, and (4) humanist.

1. Behaviourism is associated with Pavlov and Skinner. Behaviourism emphasizes the importance of objective study of an actual response; in other words, the concern is with input practice and output behaviour which is similar and measurable. The pure behaviourist is not concerned with the conscious process. A contemporary, Robert Gagné, argues that as a change in human disposition, learning cannot be associated with the process of growth (Knowles, 1984). In terms of educational practice, this means that the learner is a passive recipient and container of socio-cultural values which are transmitted by a teacher who is in control via direct instruction methods of teaching. This perspective is characterized by an overloaded syllabus and long reading lists, and it encourages a surface approach to learning (Fox, 1983). The focus is upon the transfer of knowledge and values from the learned to the learner.
2. Freud, who most people associate with psychoanalysis, was a neurologist. Learning theory which is based upon this perspective, while not so much man-as-machine orientated as behaviourism, is dependent upon the notion that growth happens as a result of resolution of conflicts at various stages in life. Change theorists, as we show in Chapter 7, regard this perspective as rather romantic and idealistic in character. In terms of teaching practice, the psychoanalytic perspective is student-centred, in

contrast to the society-centred practice of the behavioural approach to learning. Fox (1983) considers the psychoanalytic perspective to be a development from the transfer focus of behaviourism to what he calls the 'travelling theory', referring to human growth, of this second perspective.

3. The cognitive school of learning is sometimes referred to as the 'Eureka!' approach to teaching; its advocates also call this 'insight learning'. Another phrase you might hear in relation to the cognitive school is: 'The penny has dropped'. While these phrases oversimplify and generalize the cognitive field, our intention here is simply to introduce educational perspectives in relation to our theme in this book, the management of change in mental health care. The cognitive view owes its development to the considerable contributions of Piaget and Bruner, among others. It is more widely used in education than the behavioural or psychoanalytical perspectives. The cognitive perspective is also student-centred, as suggested by the popular phrases that refer to it. However, it does examine students on what they are supposed to receive from the learning experience. This pragmatic view, then, has the students shaped, as it were, by the meaning, values, and knowledge which they are intended to receive from the educational environment.
4. The humanist perspective is perhaps best characterized by the work of Carl Rogers. Here the educational process involves a change in the way learning is managed. The teaching is not based or focused upon what the teacher transmits, nor is it based upon the students' maturation; nor again is it based upon stages of intellectual development (as it is in the behaviourist, psychoanalytic, and cognitive perspectives). Rather the focus of learning with Rogerian humanists is upon understanding, empathy, and the personal growth of the student. The educational methods will be quite different here, because the teacher is not the locus of control, and learning by students is from the inside out rather than from outside in. And of course the research methods in this perspective will be quite different from those in the behaviourist perspective, for instance, where input and output variables are stressed. The humanist education view would need to be examined on the basis of its concern with creativity, growth, and change.

Table 2.1 Survey of teachers' answers to the question 'what do you mean by teaching?'

Summary sheet	*Transfer theory (behaviourist)*	*Travelling theory (psychoanalytic)*	*Shaping theory (cognitive)*	*Growing theory (humanist)*
Verbs commonly used	Convey, impart, implant, imbue, give, expound, transmit, put over, propound, tell	Lead, point the way, guide, initiate, help, show, direct, (show the way)	Develop, mould, demonstrate, produce, instruct, condition, prepare, direct (give orders)	Cultivate, encourage, nurture, develop, foster, enable, help, bring out
Subject matter	Commodity to be transferred, to fill a container	Terrain to be explored, vantage points	Shaping tools, patterns, blueprint	Experience to be incorporated into developing personality
Students	Container to be filled	Explorer	Inert material (clay, wood, metal) to be shaped	Developing personality, growing plants
Teachers	Pump attendant, food processor, barmaid	Experienced and expert travelling companion, guide, provider of travelling aids	Skilled craftsman working on raw material or selecting and assembling components	Resource provider, gardener

Standard teaching methods	Lectures, reading lists, duplicated notes	Simulations, projects, etc.; exercises with outcomes; discussions, independent learning	Laboratory, workshop, practical instructions like recipes; exercises with predictable outcomes	Experiential methods similar to travelling theory but less structured and more spontaneous
Monitoring progress	Measuring and sampling contents of vessel	Comparing notes with travelling companion	Checking size and shape of vessel	Listening to reflections on personal development
Explanations of failure – teachers' view	Leaky vessels, small container	Blinkered vision, lack of stamina, unadventurous, lethargic	Flawed, faulty material	Poor start, inadequately prepared, so unable to develop
Explanations of failure – students' view	Poor transfer skills, poor aim	Poor guides, poor equipment, too many restrictions on route	Incompetent craftsmen, poor or missing blueprint	Restricted diet, unsuitable food, incompetent gardener
Attitude to training	Need simple skills of transfer	Need skills of expert guide as well as knowledge of terrain	Need shaping to British standard teacher	Need skills of diagnosing needs of individual plants

Source: Fox (1983).

It is important to determine where one's view of a subject like education, teaching, or learning, comes from because this will determine, in turn, what kinds of question one may ask. The way one asks questions will, in turn, determine the kind of research methods to which one is attracted. Although much of general nursing education – like education throughout the UK – continues to use the cognitive school perspective, psychiatric nursing has moved to the humanist view. This is largely due to the impetus of the 1982 syllabus. The individual, whether a student or a patient, is seen as the most reliable source of knowledge about his/her own capabilities, resources, and characteristics, according to the humanist view. Naturally, this has led to experiential teaching methods and groupwork, for example, in contrast to lecture methods or programmed learning which feature in other perspectives.

The conceptual model used by Fox (1983) for thinking about the process of teaching and learning is based on how teachers respond to the question: 'what do you mean by teaching?' We can apply his four basic 'theories of teaching' to our four perspectives as shown in Table 2.1 which shows the findings of the survey of teachers' answers to the question 'what do you mean by teaching?' (from Fox, 1983). Nine categories (down the left hand side) of the question illustrate a range of four different constructs (behaviourist, psychoanalytic, cognitive, humanist) to each category. At the very least, Fox's survey demonstrates the need to enquire about educators' views of learning styles, methods and opportunities in a changing personal and social environment.

Comparison of examples of transfer, travelling, shaping, and growing theory with behaviourist, psychoanalytic, cognitive, and humanist views of learning is for the purpose of illustrating the differences between educational perspectives. Given these differences, methods of managing change in mental health care may be inappropriate if the learning environment and learning styles are not taken into account.

2.2 A SPECIFIC SITUATION: AN INNER LONDON SETTING

Local, national, and international organizations have during the past twenty-five years indicated that large institutions are inappropriate for the treatment and care of mentally ill people. Among these organizations are the World Health Authority (WHA) and the Department of Health and Social Security (DHSS), plus regional and local health authorities who are (or are in the process of) shutting psychiatric hospitals. The Hospital Advisory Service (HAS) did not report any examples of good practice inside the wards of our particular health authority's large mental hospital (HAS, 1986) – but this is not unusual. The HAS failed to find one elderly care area where long-term care was of a desirable standard, in 30 consecutive visits during four years (Horrocks, 1987). The outgoing HAS director was further quoted in the *Nursing Times* as saying that people do not have their own personalized clothing and are still put on commodes in the middle of a ward. Horrocks generalized his recent experience, deciding to omit any mention of individual visits. As far as the transition from hospital to community-based care is concerned, the Audit Commission for Local Authorities in England and Wales have conducted a survey of progress in mental handicap services. Their report, *Making a Reality of Community Care* (1986), states that most authorities are nowhere near meeting 1971 targets, let alone more recent ones. If progress in the twenty-year programme for switching services in mental handicap is anything to go by, there appear to be serious implications for local authority planners who are cutting back and closing down mental health hospital services before community services are up and running! Priority in the transition to new services is upon administration and planning, to the detriment of staff preparation for change and skills training and to the network of relationships between staff and their clients.

Within this scenario, registered mental nurses (RMNs) continue to be trained in accordance with the various curricula approved by, in our case, the English National Board for Nursing (ENB), to the criteria of the 1982 Syllabus. Post-basic training, however, is provided by either a staff development department at a school of nursing or, where none exists, an in-service training officer. These staff development teachers have been operating independent continuing education programmes, according to local needs in their respective mental health care areas. Similarly, there has never been a standard, nationwide training for nursing assistants; these courses, like many post-registration courses, have been determined by local needs. However, in addition to the 'basic' Registered Mental Nurse

(RMN) course, a number of post-basic courses are designed to a standard ENB syllabus, e.g. ENB 953, Developments in Psychiatric Nursing. Universities, colleges and polytechnics also offer ENB-approved courses. A formal training for nursing assistants is usually resisted by nursing departments, because the United Kingdom Central Council for Nursing, Midwifery and Health Visiting recognized only two levels of training (not three), namely the registered nurse training and the enrolled nurse training. As schools of nursing are receiving more autonomy to develop curricula according to their local needs, one of the ways in which they are improving education is by looking at its relevance to the local community.

Therefore, mental health units and schools of nursing are looking at the gaps in their current provision, in-service and education respectively, with a view to consumers who use the service and student carers. Educators are attempting to improve their curricula, and in our own health authority the method used is that of 'situational analysis', an examination of the cultural influences in the local community. This consists of two parts, after the model for curriculum planning by Skilbeck (1984) and Lawton (1983). Here we give a worked example to illustrate how this method measures the extent to which the curriculum is in touch with the reality of a real community. Objectives for learning can then be set to meet the needs of people in the practice setting.

2.3 EXTERNAL ANALYSIS

By 'external' analysis we refer to that external to the mental hospital. We have already mentioned in this chapter that what is learned in the nursing school is not necessarily practised on the wards. Similarly, a look at what is going on in the community will offer a measure of how relevant is the basic or post-basic education to people who use the mental health services outside of hospital. Here it is relevant that inner city life is considered because this is where psychiatric nursing care will need to be as mental hospitals are run down and their long-stay patients discharged.

An informal summary of the nurse education profile, completed for the West Lambeth borough in 1987, presents a picture of rising unemployment, increasing crime rates, and high tenant turnover in badly designed housing estates. There is a significant single-parent family population; within a borough rich in cultural diversity, new families are created from previous family separations. Anxiety, stress, loneliness, and depression are identified as health needs in the community.

Questions arise as to how a nurses' course can access itself to local people, how the local borough can be prepared for and participate in curriculum development, where no curriculum existed in the past. A curriculum has been defined as: no more than a way of expressing ideas in a form that allows those ideas to be tested in practice (Rudduck, 1984, p. 232); and 'an attempt to communicate the essential principles and features of an educational proposal in such a form that it is open to critical scrutiny and capable of effective translation into practice' (Stenhouse, 1975, p. 4).

Another issue in the external analysis of the educational situation is recognition of the professional or statutory influences upon that situation. Here as far as nursing is concerned, educational changes thought to be necessary are outlined in the Royal College of Nursing (RCN) Commission (Judge) Report (1985), The English National Board (ENB) *Strategy Paper* (1985), and the United Kingdom Central Council's (UKCC) *Project 2000* Report (1986). While proposals for an educational, collegiate base to nursing training were being formed, most psychiatric nursing schools were implementing new courses of study in accordance with the General Nursing Council (GNC) 1982 Syllabus. In addition to these external influences, there are the introduction of the General Certificate of Secondary Education, the Youth Training Scheme initiative, and use of the enrolled nurses' qualification to fulfil the entry requirement for registered nurse training. The ideology of a profession has its 'givens' or statutory requirements. These are imbued in educational processes, such as course aims and objectives. An external analysis is intended to balance these imposed values with those of new citizen-based mental health services, e.g. where the focus of care is on individuals' social functioning rather than personal pathology.

One implication arising from this external analysis of our educational situation is the changing nature of the subject-matter that is to be taught. For example, the 1982 Syllabus represents changing ideologies such as the shift from task-centred custodial care to individualized care, from cure to care, from convergent learning styles to divergent learning, and from didactic instruction in the classroom to discovery and experiential learning as a teaching method. Here a further implication provided by the analysis of community changes influencing a realistic approach to education in mental health care concerns the importance of racial issues, in a community where the total ethnic minorities' population is greater than the indigenous population.

A final issue in the external analysis for the purposes of considering educational perspectives is the growing links with local polytechnic colleges and other institutions. However, it remains to be seen whether teacher support systems will develop in this transition from nursing schools to higher education. There is no more evidence for the preparation and continuing development of teachers in their process of change than there is for the nurse practitioner in the transition from hospital to community care in mental health.

2.4 AN INTERNAL ANALYSIS OF EDUCATIONAL OPPORTUNITIES

Internal analysis of a specific situation in curriculum planning entails an examination of the students involved and their aptitudes, abilities, and defined educational needs. However, for the purpose of this discussion, it is sufficient to describe what is involved here, rather than detail examples. An internal analysis involves the contribution of nurse teachers, together with a consideration of the ethos of the school, tradition, relation with the delivery-of-care side of the organization in a health authority, and the institutional culture where a mental health service is being provided. This analysis assesses perceived and felt problems or shortcomings within the existing curriculum.

Past courses for RMNs have provided subject-centred and teacher-centred training. Today the learning environment reflects that same educational tradition in so far as custody and task-centred care continue in hospital and community settings. Key issues in the internal analysis are identifying learning styles and learning needs of future practitioners. Comparing the data of this analysis with the external-to-the-school information, and comparing learners' needs with those of local consumers, will yield a measure of the extent to which educational ideas are relevant to the needs of a mental health service.

Linking external and internal analysis of our local nursing and public community, from an educational point of view, also helps to make clear which of the perspectives, discussed in the first section of this chapter, is relevant to the here-and-now requirements of a mental health service.

In the course of the internal analysis RMN training may be examined in the light of today's needs. Our local psychiatric course examination was set to inform us what was taught; knowledge disciplines, such as sociology and anthropology, were not well defined, and learners complained they were not prepared to cope with the experiences they faced in mental health care areas. Curriculum planning using cultural and situational analysis – inside and outside the school – is a way to clarify and update courses.

Our glimpse of the ins and outs, the internal-to-the-school and external areas, such as one-parent families, preparatory to curriculum planning, brings to light current deficits in training. For example, RMN intakes in our health authority have always contained ethnic minority group members. Yet the course of training did not recognize race or culture in its curriculum subjects. However, the RMN course prescribed by the 1982 syllabus requires learning opportunities which allow for the clarification of personal values and development of self-awareness as part and parcel of acquiring skills in psychiatric nursing. In 1983, during the early days of the Management of Change Project, we found no acknowledgement that the patients were on the whole from one culture and the staff from another. For example, the in-service training timetables – like the RMN timetables – would have been illuminated by a situational and cultural analysis first, prior to planning the curriculum. Such an analysis produces evidence of the kind of educational changes required; e.g. teaching time in the curriculum for fostering multi-cultural appreciation and communications skills with facilitative teaching methods designed to enhance racial awareness.

Potentially there are contradictions in attempting to alter the status quo in nurse education as far as mental health care nursing is concerned. The professional values of nursing are embodied in its statutory bodies (see UKCC, 1986; RCN, 1985; ENB, 1985). These values may not be consistent with wide ranges of entry qualification for courses which would access prospective nurses from inner city communities. Mixed-ability teaching may lead to changes in the content of curriculum and methods of teaching and learning, which may dilute professional values. And the influence of a contemporary ideology such as normalization – that is, valuing devalued people – is contrary to the traditional ethos of psychiatric hospital nursing.

Project 2000 (UKCC, 1986) epitomizes current professional educational values in nursing, with its initiative for higher learning opportunities. At the very least, this will result in formal links with colleges of further education and universities across Britain. It is a refreshing experience in our health authority to see nurse educators trying to balance and synthesize the needs of a profession with the needs of a community.

Situational and cultural analysis in curriculum planning enables teachers to match educational perspectives with local community needs, learning styles, changes in the provision of services, and many other aspects of arranging courses of training or further education. One important final point is the relevance of this type of planning to action research. The educator Lawrence Stenhouse was probably the first person in Britain to introduce this notion of action research. A teacher is a person who uses research in the process of teaching: the use of findings is the action of research in classrooms, or other places where learning occurs. The aims of action research were, therefore, to promote the quality of teaching practice, to promote the development of practical theory, and to promote the development of teacher status. The framework of this new research model incorporates both the finding out and the improving characteristics of any research proposal. The framework also includes the characteristics of change and reflection. Action research combines the purposes of research with the community and school needs of teachers and learners. As with the nature of cultural and situational analysis in curriculum planning, action research is the study of a situation with a view to improving it. This kind of planning and research underpins both the thinking and practice illustrated in the chapters which follow. Inside this framework is the process of finding out and identifying, reflecting and clarifying, acting, formulating, and disseminating. The present book puts flesh on the bones of this cyclical process, in the field of continuing mental health care education.

2.5 LEARNING AND CHANGE

Personal change is inherent in learning. The philosophical forefather of the cognitive school of learning, Dewey, argues that education supplies the very conditions which ensure growth, or adequacy, of life (Dewey, 1961). In Table 2.2 definitions of learning side by side with change also illustrate the mutual closeness of these two concepts.

Thinking about learning and change in the comparative ways of the last two sections of this chapter, it is clear that teaching methods and learning styles in mental health care must address the issue of how personal change and individual growth relate to practical skills, or competencies. The methods of the educational process must then be consistent with these criteria, if the outcomes, whether anticipated change in attitudes or a patient's rehabilitation success, are to be realistic. Therefore, change is a central, although neglected, concept within education as well as being more obvious (from a situational analysis, for example) as a central feature in the emergent mental health services of the twenty-first century. In terms of teaching methods, it could be argued that the reflective process of learning (Boud *et al.*, 1985, pp. 20, 27, 36) which could encompass this thinking is only available through the humanist perspective of education (see Fig. 2.1).

Table 2.2 Definitions of learning and change

Learning	*Change*
Any change in an individual that expresses itself in a relatively stable form of behaviour, and which is the result of an interaction with the environment, mediated by the senses. (Borger and Seaborne, 1982, p. 13)	A generic term embracing a family of concepts, e.g. innovation, development, renewal. Innovation is an intentional process, while change can also include accidental or unintentional movements or shifts. (Bolam, 1975, p. 279)
A change in a person that comes about as a result of experience. Learning is an internal change in a person, the formation of new associations, or the potential for	One fundamental assumption underlying empirical strategies for changing is that men will follow their rational self-interest once

Table 2.2 (*Continued*)

Learning	*Change*
new responses. It is a relatively permanent change in a person's capabilities. (Woolfolk and McCune-Nicolich, 1984, pp. 159, 161) The apparent modification of a person's behaviour through his activities and experiences, so that his knowledge, skills, and attitudes, including modes of adjustment, toward his environment are changed, more or less permanently. (Curzon, 1985, p. 14) Learning takes place at a very great pace, when the newborn child does not distinguish himself from others or from other things. Then, after six months, a 'not-self' emerges. Learning is involved in change, but the meaning of learning is important in the (whole-life) developmental framework. (Rayner, 1978, pp. 35–8) Being part of a society, with that society trying somehow to keep the error rate down to a minimum by arranging manageable encounters. (Bruner, 1983, p. 41)	this is revealed to them. A third assumption about human motivation is framed in re-education strategy. According to this view, change in the normal orientation of a person requires changes in attitudes, values, skills, and significant relationships (not just changes in knowledge, information, or intellectual rationales for action and practice). (Chinn and Benne, 1985, p. 23) There seems to be little difference between education and development in relation to sequential change. (Hirst and Peters, 1970, p. 57)

2.6 RECOGNITION OF CHANGE

Today situational and cultural analysis in curriculum planning of mental health care nursing make a strong statement about the need

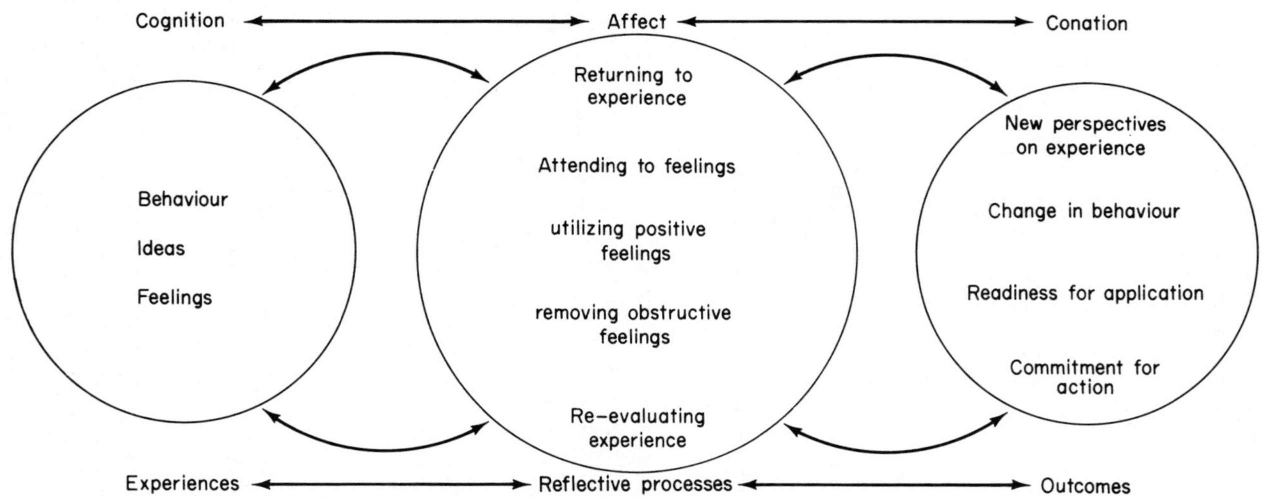

Fig. 2.1 The reflective process in a context of learning (from Boud *et al.*, 1985, pp. 20, 27, 36).

for educational change. The reason for this would appear to be related to the development of culture. Culture, whether in south London generally or one of its mental hospitals, is not static, but changes and develops with the character and environment inhabited by its people. Ideological shifts in the late twentieth century (such as more personal freedoms, individual responsibility, equal opportunity, and environmental protection) are the seeds which connect humanist growth in individuals with change in their cultures. In terms of professional accountability in mental health care nursing, respect for clients' rights and choices and lifestyle has confirmed the rise of humanism. Both the argument and the evidence is becoming stronger against new-style management in the 1980s, when economic consideration by managers is more important than the human needs of people who use mental health services. Here appropriate educational and managerial processes are not integrated, but separate perspectives which split the pulp of care delivery right to its heart, like the lumberjack with his wood axe making short work of stumps for firewood.

Change and learning are key ingredients in an educational process which connect personal growth with social skills, in curricula for mental health care. The teaching and learning mechanism is illustrated by the example in Fig. 2.1, although others have been mentioned in the discussion of educational perspectives. However, learning is more multi-dimensional than can be accounted for by the psychologists who influenced theory. Change theory provides evidence that the social and environmental dimensions to learning are also an important influence upon an educational perspective, or intended learning outcome.

At least one apparent invariable aspect of modern times is the tendency to change; perhaps this has always been an invariant? Certainly, it has always been an invariant in the human organism, for example, in the process of physical growth and ageing. Apart from this, Bennis, Benne and Chinn (1985) see two pathways to change. One they call the 'law of non-intervention'. This is the 'invisible hand' ideology of the *laissez-faire* doctrine. The second pathway to change is the 'law of radical intervention', represented by the opposite extreme to non-intervention by Marxist analysis. Chinn and Benne (1985) identify three types of strategy which illustrate these pathways to change (Table 2.3). The first group in this illustration is the empirical-rational group of strategies. This group assumes that people are rational and that they will follow their

Table 2.3 Strategies of deliberate changing (from Chinn and Benne, 1985, pp. 44–5)

Rational/empirical	*Normative/re-educative*	*Power/coercive*
(Views of the Enlightenment and classical liberalism)	(Views of therapists, trainers, and situation changers)	(Use of political institutions)
Basic research and dissemination of knowledge through general education	Improving the problem-solving capabilities of a system	Strategies of non-violence (e.g. strikes, negotiations)
Personnel selection and replacement	Releasing and fostering growth in the persons who make up the system to be changed	Use of political institutions (e.g. ballot laws, judicial decisions)
Systems analysts as staff consultants		Changing through the recomposition and manipulation of power élites
Applied research and linkage systems for diffusion of research results	Freud (psychotherapy)	(Non-violent strategies) Gandhi
Utopian thinking as a strategy of changing	Rogers (counselling)	Martin Luther King
Perceptual and conceptual reorganization through the clarification of language	Lewin (research, training, action)	(Changing power élites) Marx

rational self-interest once it is revealed to them! The second type of change strategy is the normative/re-educative. Here man interacts with his environment. Effective innovation requires a change of attitudes, relationships, values, and skills. Therefore, the activity within and among people involves change agents. (For a further discussion see p. 175.)

The use of power is instrumental in all three strategies of change. In the rational–empirical, knowledge is the major ingredient of power; the normative/re-educative strategies 'recognise the importance of noncognitive determinants of behaviour as resistances or supports to changing – values, attitudes, and feelings at the personal level and norms and relationships at the social level' (Chinn and Benne, 1985, p. 23); the power–coercive strategies emphasize political and economic sanctions in the exercise of power.

The innovator of change theory, social psychologist Kurt Lewin, argues that the processes by which we acquire the normal and abnormal are similar (Chinn and Benne, 1985). There are common themes running through education, or rehabilitation for that matter, whether you are a human services worker in mental health care (e.g. a nurse) or a user of services. Regardless of who we are or what our behaviour is like, forward movement and growth involves changes in thinking, feeling, and doing – as does backwards movement. Examples of backwards movement might be professional misconduct, or a challenging behaviour which is socially unacceptable – an act of violence to a client, for instance.

One may also perceive this movement to and fro in the changing constructions put upon the concept of mental illness. Such is the uncertainty about defining mental illness that the authors of the latest Mental Health Act avoided it! The Mental Health Unit in our own health authority defines it as a 'learning difficulty'. The change from multi-disciplinary working to interdisciplinary working has further widened recognition of the changing views of what mental illness is. Now on some mental health teams all disciplines are not represented; during the days of multi-disciplinary working this would be unheard of. From one member of the interdisciplinary team, one might hear mental illness referred to as 'regression'; from another member the word 'psychotic' may be uttered; yet another member may refer to the person using the mental health service as a 'devalued person in a devalued environment'. A major illness, which might be called schizophrenia by a medical doctor, might be referred to by a nurse, who may or may not be an academic doctor, as a loss of differentiation of the self. Regardless of their practical or academic progress, nursing diagnosis would be specific to the individual rather than generalized across a population of service users.

The notion of change being retro-active or pro-active can be illustrated using the nursing diagnosis referred to above. The loss of differentiation of the self can be likened to an infant child who has not yet matured enough to tell the difference between himself and anything else; there is only himself at first. Similarly, serious mental illness can be seen as a backward-moving change such that the mature self misplaces the ability to remain self-secure and moves back and forth to the extent that, in a frank loss of reality (what has commonly been called psychosis or, even less validly, lunacy), there is no differentiation between self and anything else. Considering such movements in personality, for the purposes of thinking of change and learning in the other, the client, it may become understandable that the educational perspective for mental health care students should include experience of and skilled sensitivity to the possibility of such change in the helper, the nurse. Therefore, the reflective process (see Fig. 2.1) demands that the nurse's backward and forward experience be examined as part of the self-assessment in personal growth and learning.

If it is true that there is this backward and forward movement in personality which involves learning, growth, and coping with change, then it would seem that learning is reversible, and the abnormality would be called mental illness by some and learning, growth, or coping difficulties by others. Essentially, therefore, the problem becomes a learning difficulty which, by its very nature, involves adaptation to a cultural and social situation. Perhaps this is why Lewin refers to adult learning as 're-education' rather than learning or education? The nurse's task, by this reasoning, would seem to be one of helping to re-learn, to regain, to retain growth – a process involving change which the nurse and client experience together in re-education.

The difference between learning and motivation is problematic; however, motivation plays an important role in learning (Einon, 1981). If as Peplau (1952) maintains the nurse's use of language is the only controlled and appropriate stimuli, a client's responses to words may enhance or reverse a backwards change by language use which energizes a learning deficit where motivation appears, at least on the surface, to be the crippling factor; Goldstein (1981) refers to motivation as the energy of learning and change. Why people choose to pursue or refrain from pursuing a goal becomes a crucial question to the actual changed experience. The relation of motivation to learning and change arises from the etymological root of emotion and motive: they both derive from *motus*, 'to move'.

Whether people are helpers, users of a service, or learners, issues of incentive, self-determination, and personal rights become important to the educational support they receive and to the mental health system in their community. Here these issues are crucial because an educational perspective must be able to account for how able it is to address these issues for people providing a caring service, which involves teaching, learning, change, and growth, both in the service provider and the service user. Having examined some of the baselines for an educational perspective in mental health care, we now turn to the question of how this might look in action, using research in a supporting but essential role to determine the direction and meaning of our work.

REFERENCES

Audit Commission for Local Authorities in England and Wales (1986) *Making a Reality of Community Care*, HMSO, London.

Beck, C., Rawlins, R. and Williams, S. (eds) (1984) *Mental Health Care – Psychiatric Nursing: A Holistic Life-cycle Approach*, C.V. Mosby, St Louis, MO.

Benne, K. (1985) The processes of re-education: an assessment of Kurt Lewin's views, in W.E. Bennis *et al. The Planning of Change*, 4th edn, Holt, Rinehart and Winston, New York, pp. 272–311.

Bennis, W.G., Benne, K.D. and Chinn, R. (eds) (1985) *The Planning of Change*, 4th edn, Holt, Rinehart and Winston, New York.

Bolam, R. (1975) The management of educational change: towards a conceptual framework, in A. Harris, M. Lawn and W. Prescott, (eds) *Curriculum Innovation*, Croom Helm, London, pp. 273–90.

Borger, R. and Seaborne, A. (1982) *The Psychology of Learning*, 2nd edn, Penguin, Harmondsworth.

Boud, D., Keogh, R., and Walker, D. (eds) (1985) *Reflection: Turning Experience into Learning*, Kogan Page, London.

Bruner, J. (1983) The growth of cognitive psychology: developmental psychology, in J. Miller, (ed.) *States of Mind*, BBC, London, pp. 30–41.

Chinn, R. and Benne, K.D. (1985) General strategies for effecting changes in human systems, in W.G. Bennis, *et al.* (eds) *The Planning of Change*, 4th edn, Holt, Rinehart and Winston, New York, pp. 22–45.

Curzon, C.B. (1985) *Teaching in Further Education: An Outline of Principles and Practice*, 3rd edn, Holt, Rinehart and Winston, New York.

Department of Health and Social Security (1985) *Mental Illness Hospitals and Units in England: Results from the Mental Health Enquiry* 1983, DHSS, London.

Dewey, J. (1961) *Education and Democracy*, The Free Press, New York.

Einon, G. (ed.) (1981) *Motivation: Biology and Brain Behaviour*, Open University Press, Milton Keynes.

English National Board for Nursing, Midwifery and Health Visiting (ENB) (1985) *Professional Education/Training Courses*, ENB, London.

Fox, D. (1983) Personal theories of teaching. *Studies in Higher Education* **8**(2), 151–63.

General Nursing Council (1982) *Training Syllabus: Register of Nurses for Mental Nursing*, GNC, London.

Goldstein, H. (1981) *Social Learning and Change: A Cognitive Approach to Human Services*, Tavistock, London.

Hirst, P.H. and Peters, R.S. (1970) *The Logic of Education*, Routledge and Kegan Paul, London.

Horrocks, P. (1987) HAS condems standards of long-term care. *Nursing Times*, 20 May, 10.

Hospital Advisory Service (HAS) (1986) *The Report of a Visit to a South London Hospital*, HAS, Beckenham.

Jarvis, P. (1983) *Adult and Continuing Education*, Croom Helm, London.

Kerr, J.F. (1968) *Changing the Curriculum,*, University of London Press, London.

Kitson, A.L. (1986) Indicators of quality in nursing care – an alternative approach. *Journal of Advanced Nursing* **11**, 133–44.

Knowles, M. (1984) *The Adult Learner: A Neglected Species*, 3rd edn, Gulf Publishing, London.

Laing, R.D. (1965) *The Divided Self – an Existential Study in Sanity and Madness*, Penguin, Harmondsworth.

Lawton, D. (1983) *Curriculum Studies and Educational Planning*, Hodder and Stoughton, London.

Mezirow, J. (1981) A critical theory of adult learning and evaluation. *Adult Education* **31**(1), 3–24.

Peplau, H. (1952) *Interpersonal Relations in Nursing: A Conceptual Frame of Reference for Psychodynamic Nursing*, G.P. Putnam, New York.

Rayner, E. (1978) *Human Development: An Introduction to the Psychodynamics of Growth, Maturity and Ageing*, 2nd edn, Allen and Unwin, London.

Rogers, C. (1983) *Freedom to Learn for the 80's*, 2nd edn, Charles Merrill.

Royal College of Nursing (1985) *The Education of Nurses: A New Dispensation* (Judge Report), RCN, London.

Rudduck, J. (1984) Curriculum Development and Teacher Research, in M. Skilbeck, (ed.) *Readings in School-Based Curriculum Development* Ch 22, Harper and Row, London, pp. 231–43.

Schall, M.S. (1983) Communication-rules approach to organization culture. *Administrative Science Quarterly* **28**, 557–81.

Skilbeck, M. (ed.) (1984) *Evaluating the Curriculum in the Eighties*, Hodder and Stoughton, London.

Stenhouse, L. (1975) *An Introduction to Curriculum Research and Development*, Heinemann, London.

United Kingdom Central Council for Nursing, Midwifery and Health Visiting (UKCC) (1986) *Project 2000: A New Preparation for Practice*, UKCC, London.

Woolfolk, A. and McCune-Nicolich, L. (1984) *Educational Psychology for Teachers*, 2nd edn, Prentice-Hall, Englewood Cliffs, NJ.

World Health Organization (1979) *Nursing Service: Report on a WHO Symposium, Stuttgart, 1978*, WHO, Copenhagen.

— 3 —
Actioning change through research

3.1 INTRODUCTION

This chapter describes the origins of a particular problem, identifies the questions and issues, and examines the use of an action research framework involving a group of shopfloor nurses in bringing about change. We describe an institutional setting, traditional approaches to staffing, the culture and how these block learning. Motivation is explored as the key to actioning change, together with the implications for training and change.

Here we describe the background to the Management of Change Project. Coinciding with this local project are those shared themes of the western world of today, of devolution in mental health services to community bases, client participation, and de-institutionalization. In this context, the chapter will address the questions of what kind of action, what kind of change, and what kind of research will have an impact on a mental hospital culture which handicaps motivation and change. The local educational dilemma of how to prepare staff in a mental hospital for the major social changes, which are the themes of the mental health services today, will be identified.

First, the setting. Tooting Bec is a Victorian-built institution, the sheer size of which is a testament to the rise of the medical profession, discussed in Chapter 1. Overlooking Tooting Bec Common in south London, the hospital is surrounded by high walls. There is an imposing iron gate and caged walkways which connect the dormitory-like buildings at first- and second-floor levels.

During the Management of Change Project (1983–6) there were 864 beds, 70% of which were for the over 65s. During the project there were 73 patient vacancies and 60 staff vacancies.

On an elderly care ward, first thing in the morning, a lady is pushed in a chair across a room at such speed that she misinterprets the nurse's action for aggression. The nurse offers no verbal explanation for this action. The lady strikes out at the nurse with her elbow and, turning slightly in the wheelchair, manages to punch the air behind in the direction of the nurse. The nurse – focused on her task of getting the patient from A to B so as to return to dress and convey the next person from bed to breakfast table – has demonstrated an example of typical institutional behaviour, where concern with the task has become, imperceptibly and without conscious thought, more important than concern for the person.

3.2 STAFFING INSTITUTIONS

Traditionally the managers of British asylums and mental hospitals have depended on untrained nurses to provide the hands and muscle to cope with the elderly people who are out of touch with the reality of the everyday world. The middle-aged mentally ill person has for many years been resident in these institutions where they have been sheltered and fed. Today this attitude of staffing towards the less acute areas of psychiatry, where the less valued, lower-priority clients such as the elderly and long-stay persons are found, is typified in the number of nursing assistants in the five-ward area that we studied and worked with.

The Management of Change Project demonstrated that an enrolled nurse was in charge from 40% to 58% of the time, that is a registered six-month period in 1985, 47% of the time. The fact that this varied so much between the five wards is indicative of the inconsistent system of staffing the hospital. There is no establishment quota per ward of nurses and no assessment system of clients to determine their staffing needs *vis-à-vis* the number of nurses required for a standard of care. Standards of care remained undefined. The enrolled nurses and nursing assistants were regularly taken away without notice and without sister's approval. These enrolled nurses and nursing assistants were the people who clients knew personally and recognized, even in their apparent confusion and disorientation.

This, at a time when, for more than twenty-five years, international, national, regional, district, and local bodies have advocated de-institutionalizing mental health services. However, there is little, if any, indication in *Hospital Services for the Mentally Ill* (DHSS 1971) or *The Way Forward* (DHSS 1977) of either the value of initiatives in education involving shopfloor nurses upwards, rather than from the boardroom down, or that preparation of staff and clients was more important than administrative decisions to close mental hospitals.

3.3 THE CULTURAL BLOCK TO LEARNING

In the early 1980s the 150 nursing assistants who worked in the adult mental illness unit of West Lambeth Health Authority rotated through a basic two-week and a later one-week refresher course conducted in the nursing school. We found in evaluating this training scheme that while the acquisition of skills had occurred in an unthinking way, the conscious conversion of this learning did not occur. There was no evidence in the nursing assistants' behaviour, on their return to the ward, that they had made the transition from the acquiring of skills to using them. The curriculum for this training was changed six times, until eventually one-third of their course was conducted on the wards among their own ward teams. However, the outcome remained the same, namely that once working on the wards, the nursing assistants did not use the skills that they had been taught.

It became clear that learning did not occur in an environment which does not experience change, a place which Barton (1959) describes as 'deadening'. Similarly, it is a place where Vernon (1971) would deduce that perception becomes so blunted that the process of seeing is complete before incoming stimuli (such as conversation) start.

If learning does occur in these environments, it is not consistent with the kind of change which is compatible with a therapeutic environment; that is, an environment which would support a change from custodial task-centred nursing to individualized patient-centred care characterized by problem-solving attitudes in nurses' values. But, as Shainberg (1983) puts it: 'You can only change something when you know what it is . . . when you are connected with it experientially and once you see how you live it and how you create it' (p. 52). Therefore, there is a type of learning which perpetuates an institutionalized custody-oriented culture. People who work and reside in mental institutions tend to become carriers of such values in a culture; Goffman (1961) describes these values in his book *Asylums*.

Observation is the *sine qua non* of the behavioural sciences; it is the main method of collecting data, according to Dobson *et al.* (1981). That this is the process which becomes blunted in institutional care makes even more ironical our finding that nurses' beliefs about their practice are contrary to their own eventual perceptions, shared by ourselves, a researcher, and a teacher.

By looking at the ward culture closely, using participant observation and structured interviews, involving all 78 staff working on the five wards, it was evident that the nursing assistants, not the sisters, were in control of the wards. (Of the 58 day staff, 43% were nursing assistants, 10% learners, 29% enrolled nurses, and 18% ward sisters.) The hospital's dependence on the nursing assistant staff grade is illustrated by the extent of:

1. Manning the elderly care areas with them;
2. Arbitrarily pulling them out of one ward to compensate for absence in another;
3. Amending sister's off-duty, in those cases where sister was given the token authority of arranging it;
4. The practice of off-duty being arranged directly with the manager instead of the sister.

This had the effect of trained staff allowing nursing assistants' practice – as described, above, in the mild form of the nurse's motor response without explanation being misinterpreted – to continue. Another example is that of the level of delivery of care being at the bottom of the hierarchy, i.e. the nursing assistant being the lowest, and the director of nursing the highest. Despite there being eight grades in the hierarchy, the standards of care were determined at the bottom of the organization, not the top.

Therefore, we decided that a bottom–up approach to finding out answers was needed, the questions being:

1. What methods can be used to create a therapeutic environment in which appropriate learning can occur, one which corrects the negative effects of an institutional culture?

2. How can such changes, from custody to person-centred and problem-solving care, be measured?
3. How does one evaluate such a process of change and get to grips with their outcome effects on client's care?
4. What organizational change is necessary and how do you go about achieving it?
5. How does learning by conscious thinking overtake the unconscious acquisition of skills?

It appeared to us that people learned skills, and these were perceived to perpetuate the routines and object relationships. These practices were counterproductive and ultimately damaging to the recipients of care.

3.4 MOTIVATION: THE KEY

From the baseline of these observations and interviews in the early 1980s, we moved the focus from that on the nursing assistants to the role of the ward sister in the mid-1980s. We needed to explore the underlying issues in actioning change through research, namely the question of motivation in the context of institutional culture.

Rituals and routines which pervade traditional mental hospitals have led us to the assumption that change within such cultures must be actioned in a way that leads to the development of new attitudes. Unless personal change and growth towards a professional maturity occurs, then it will not be possible for learning to occur, and consequently there will be a lack of understanding of the need for individuality in each client's nursing care. Basic course learners and students of registered mental nursing, together with pupils of enrolled mental nursing, have consistently complained that 'what we learn in school is different to that which we experience on the wards' – in what has become an ironic, contradictory addage in mental hospitals.

Traditionally service motivation has always been a strong power input for the nursing profession (Dickoff and James, 1968). Three motivational problems inherent in continuing service education situations are identified by O'Connor (1982, p. 13):

1. participation
2. active learning
3. application.

From these, the following assumptions arise. First, education represents change. Second, change can be threatening to one's self-esteem, and possibly to one's job security, particularly if performance in relation to the change is a basis for job-related evaluation. Third, threats to job security are threats to basic security needs.

If these assumptions are correct, it becomes essential for educational design – how teaching is conducted and under what circumstances – to fit in with peoples' perceptions and attitudes towards:

1. their needs and expectations
2. their intentions and performance
3. what exists, or should exist, to enable people to make the desired change where it inevitably clashes with the expected change.

Dickoff and James (1968) identify three main issues:

1. How can service motivation be inculcated, sustained, or increased?
2. How is service motivation decreased, inhibited, or even extinguished?
3. What are the reliable sources of motivation other than service motivation? e.g. where do people's satisfaction about work come from and how are they altered by experiencing the service?

Service motivation has been perpetuated by the culture being orientated to practices of staffing the mental hospital according to needs of nurses rather than those of patients. Since the 1970s this had wrecked the control and the authority invested in the ward sister's role. Contemporary professional psychiatric nursing seeks change by employing the old hierarchical methods of the use of power, for example, the consolidation of wards at Tooting Bec Hospital as part of cost-cutting measures and the rationalization of treatment which have denied ward staff control.

As Dickoff and James have asked, what kind of agents can be expected to have service motivation as an important power source, and what can serve to supplement or support service motivation or even stand in its stead? The Management of Change Project at Tooting Bec Hospital has answered that, in its stead; there should be stated nursing values, not hospital or institutional values, along with specific individualized standards of practice and care. These should exist together with opportunities for practitioners to learn personal and professional skills, to acquire knowledge, and to practise procedures informed by the continuing education process that has supported the project. We will talk about what happened during this process a little later in the book, in discussing how research marries with practice to create change opportunities (see Chapter 6).

Historically nursing has satisfied the lower-level needs and goals of nurses, namely the basic physiological needs of safety and security (Berns, 1982). Reviewing a number of studies on job satisfaction, Berns concludes that the most important characteristic that nurses look for in a job is the opportunity for professional growth – the need for self-actualization. This means, she argues, increased challenge, continuing education, autonomy, variety, responsibility, and respect. Therefore, educational change within organizations must create an environment which satisfies the primary needs of nurses, thereby helping them to move on to higher needs, self-fulfilment, and higher standards of patient care. Presumably educational change, what people are taught, what they learn, what happens in the process, and what outcome clients experience as a result, will fail even to raise its head unless it is deliberately designed first to tackle years of educational neglect in an unchanging environment. In the process of these years institutional education has not been about change, but rather to perpetuate a medical model of nursing. It has been about meeting basic needs and surviving mundane institutional life. An odd aspect of such a hypothesis would be that some nurses working in a mental hospital would actually say that they are completely happy.

Nurses are our clients. We listen to their words as part of our observation. It is somewhat like nursing a family in a psychotherapeutic community such as the Cassel Hospital in Surrey. Here one would not directly intervene between mother and child, but would nurse the child through the mother. Similarly, our relationship with patients at Tooting Bec Hospital is largely through the nurses. Our work could then be described as largely process and educative work with the outcome to be determined by measures of the status and records of patients. (This again we will take up later on.) One listens not just to the words, but also to the feelings which are being conveyed. In this way, we facilitate a greater wholeness in people. It is the process of accepting as valid and without commentary all of our thoughts and feelings which frees us from the conflict of wanting to be more and different than we are (Shainberg, 1983). Yet today the nurse's Code of Conduct (UKCC, 1984) clearly expects nurses to be accountable and responsible for the quality and standard of their work. Thus our input needs to be a careful balance between enabling the personal and professional growth of staff and ensuring the growth to maturity of our patients and clients. This is achieved by designing an educational approach to change which captures the perceptions and attitudes of people and acknowledges what it is to recognize what needs to be.

In Britain, introduction of the nursing process is a reflection of the change from the traditional, ritualistic approach to a more enquiring, scientific approach based on the individual's needs (Wright, 1984).

3.5 NURSING ASSISTANTS TO WARD SISTERS

It is claimed in the nursing literature that patient allocation is a better method of organizing the delivery of care than task allocation because it results in (Metcalfe, 1983):

1. improved patient care
2. greater job satisfaction for nurses
3. an improved nurse–patient relationship

Task allocation has been compared to 'assembly line working' and 'bureaucratic organization' because task allocation (e.g. baths, observations, mouth care, dressings, back rounds) is viewed as reducing care to a set of tasks performed. Metcalfe points out that what has affected the acceptability of this system of organizing the delivery of nursing care are the following trends:

1. Emphasis on the importance of the psycho-social aspects of illness, which has resulted in an emphasis on individual needs;
2. The increasing 'professionalism' of nursing, which maintains that nurses are not the 'handmaidens' of the doctors, but rather that they are, or should be, able to accept and exercise responsibility, autonomy, and decision making in their own area of expertise, namely nursing care.

Task-centred nursing does not entirely ignore the individuality of its patients, but reduces their significance and, above all, the individuality of nurses (Martin, 1984). Martin points out that Menzies (1960) has shown, with the utmost clarity, how task-centred nursing can be used to share and reduce the individual responsibility of nurses; others, such as Towell and Harries (1979), have shown how the performance of tasks can be seen as the prime function of nurses and almost a substitute for treatment. As recently as 1981, the Royal College of Nursing remarked that 'many people still see nursing as a collection of tasks or procedures'. You may remember from the historical perspective in Chapter 1 how this task-oriented perspective was described as 'depersonalizing' in that it blunts perception and imposes a handicap on critical thinking or problem-solving.

3.6 TRAINING NEEDS

The Management of Change Project which has focused on the ward sisters at Tooting Bec Hospital began in 1983 with the evaluation by a newly appointed in-service training officer of one- and two-week training courses for the 150 nursing assistants of West Lambeth Health Authority. The major problems posed by this evaluation are as follows:

1. There is no significant indication in the nursing assistant's practice that the training has taken place; their practice conformed to custodial standards of care observed prior to their training. Probably this was not unique to nursing assistants, but our hypothesis was that it would hold true for any grade of psychiatric nurse 'trained' away from the socio-environmental context (their ward), and especially so if segregated from their team colleagues;
2. The second problem posed by the nursing assistants' training course evaluation was that no systematic methods existed of collecting information to substantiate either the rationale for the training courses or the evaluation of them;
3. It became clear to the in-service training officer (in the process of slow change of the nursing assistants' training curriculum away from school-based to ward-based teaching, involving the trained staff) that all grades of staff were involved in working at the same level as the nursing assistants. Also the role of the trained staff, and particularly of the ward sister, needed recognition as being different to that of the untrained staff; furthermore, it seemed trained staff required updated skills, as well as support from the senior nurse group, in strengthening their role and regaining the authority necessary to manage their wards;

4. As one may deduce from Towell's (1975) work, the social and environmental circumstances of working in the mental hospital play a large part in determining the educational effectiveness of training. Therefore, the Management of Change Project would need to result in organizational change as well as educational and management input. Indeed organizational change is at the heart of Kurt Lewin's concept of 'action research'. (These issues are discussed in detail in Chapters 5 and 7.)

The above, then, were the problems that formed the basis of the questions for us to answer. This led to a research-based project designed not to test the hypotheses, or possible answers, but to address issues of responsibility for care, continuity of care, and individuality of care. Nursing assistants' training was discontinued and, in its place, an educational evaluative study was set up. It was designed to foster a problem-solving attitude in nurses, and to examine problems in changing from custodial, task-centred care to patient-centred, individualized care. Therefore, the project title, Management of Change, reflects not only the valued change to individualized care under the direction and control of a ward sister, but also the changes in transition from the hospital to a community-based nursing service.

While the methods of investigation will be addressed in Chapter 5, the key questions on which the interviews and questionnaires were based are as follows:

1. What are the attitudes and perceptions of the nurses on these five wards?
2. How have these attitudes and perceptions changed as a result of educational intervention?
3. How has the project affected standards and practices of care?

Typically the measures we used to attempt to answer these questions were administered before and after six months of groupwork. The process of using groupwork as a focus for the project, including the use of a group as a research instrument, is developed in Chapter 4.

3.7 COMPONENTS OF CHANGE

Ward and Moran (1984) refer to Zaltman and Duncan's (1977) definition of resistance:

> any conduct that serves to maintain the status quo in the face of pressures to alter that status . . . Habits, complacency, fear of disorganisation, set patterns of response to change, conservatism, perceived loss of current or meaningful relationships, perceived lack of rewards . . . all of these stimulate resistance to movement in any direction. (Ward and Moran, 1984, p. 30)

These writers identify the symptoms of resistance, visible in the Management of Change Project, as well as positive aspects of resistance, i.e. those signals which aid and support planned change.

People display resistance both in overt and covert ways – sometimes by displacing their frustration altogether in a transference of negative feelings on to a member of the project team. In fact we would be identified as change agents; e.g. 'You are blocking my work' or 'I have been here twenty-seven years and this idea just won't work'. But most frequent are the covert signs of resistance, manifested in delaying tactics like being late or disorganized; e.g. 'I forgot we were meeting today' or 'She wrote me a note to accompany you today but I am alone, so I couldn't come' or 'it just slipped my mind'. Perhaps most frequently this resistance is displayed by nurses being late for work.

If resistance is not recognized and dealt with by supporting the change process, Ward and Moran argue, it may become so overwhelming that it is fatal to the work. Because we identified resistance very early, it was important in the design of our work that there should be a participatory framework for enquiry, feedback, and action, so that the values people held would form the basis of understanding the difference between the beliefs of nurses and the observation of others.

Hollingworth's (1985) review of the problems in change makes several points:

1. Educational deprivation/weak knowledge base
2. Myths about change
3. Rut of experience
4. Anticipation of change with severe anxiety
5. The belief that learning by experience is better than education
6. Lack of sufficient data on which to base change
7. The normative behaviour of women.

These are among the key issues presented in the literature as being the problems of change. Hollingworth agrees with others (Allen and Murrell, 1978) in her view that:

Once one starts to question the basis of accepted and valued techniques, procedures, method and content, one pulls away trusted props, which tend to cause individuals to be threatened and anxious. This creates uncertainty, and may lead to the strengthening of existing attitudes and beliefs.
(Hollingworth, 1985, p.52)

The primary effect of change, then, as Hollingworth points out, is on people. The prerequisites of successful change are identified as support, involvement, and evaluation.

While we found that there was little autonomy and ability to participate in the decision-making on the five wards, Larson *et al.* (1984) related these two qualities to job satisfaction and quality of care. However, job satisfaction and quality of work do not correlate directly, and the reasons for this are poorly understood; as Larson puts it:

It may be that the propensity to deliver quality care is more an ethical decision or personality characteristic. It would be interesting to know if nurses who give high quality patient care are also likely to be more competent and thoughtful parents, spouses, friends, community members and so on.
(Larson *et al.*, 1984, p. 32)

Perhaps these are reasons that nursing assistants command respect by trained nurses, to the detriment of both the quality of caring and standards of nursing and the outcome of care, for combined with the institutional problems militating against individualized care, as we have already pointed out (see also Chapter 1), it is not surprising that task-centred nursing is so entrenched a symbol of custodial perceptions and attitudes. The survey in Annadale-Steiner (1979) found that waste in nursing is due to the demanding nature of the work and stresses related to it, job dissatisfaction being the largest problem. Most nurses believed that they were looking after patients' physiological needs and neglected their psychological needs. By 1986 some of the five ward teams in the project critically examined this, and identified not only the lack of resources in an impoverished environment, but also using the problem-solving processes in Quality Circles* demonstrated a paucity of thinking in the way the hospital in south London was staffed.

* A regular meeting of a group from a particular homogeneous work area who follow a set of principles in the approach to identifying and solving issues and problems to do with that work area.

To conclude, the way change is approached, and the kind of action on which change is based, are seen by us to be instrumental in effecting attitudes and perceptions which form the basis of skills in mental health nursing and the inappropriate learning we found inherent in an institutional mental hospital culture.

The Management of Change Project has aimed to evaluate attitude and role perceptions, to measure change, and to use the data as a baseline for future change and develop standards of nursing and care on five psychogeriatric wards. This study has monitored group processes, and changes towards individualized care have been noted, along with an increase in the continuity of care, and more responsibility for care has shifted back to the qualified staff, in particular, the ward sister. A new nursing development team has been used as a catalyst to form a new educational programme for basic statutory nurse learners and trained staff together on 'model wards', combining the findings of the 1983–6 project with a model for change. This prepares staff for the future in transitions from hospital to the community and, at the same time, meets the needs of institutionalized people. Exactly how this position was reached will be explained in subsequent chapters.

REFERENCES

Allen, H.O. and Murrell, J. (1978) *Nurse Training*. MacDonald Evans.

Annadale-Steiner, D. (1979) Why nurses leave: unhappiness is the nurse who expected more. *Nursing Mirror*, **22**, 34–6.

Barton, R. (1959) *Institutional Neurosis*, John Wright and Sons, London.

Berns, J.S. (1982) The application of job satisfaction theory to the nursing profession. *Nursing Leadership*, **5**(1), March, 27–33.

DHSS (1971) *Hospital Services for the Mentally Ill*, HMSO, London.

DHSS (1977) *The Way Forward*, HMSO, London.

Dickoff, J. and James, P. (1968) A theory of theories: a position paper. *Nursing Research* **17**(3) May–June, 197–203.

Dobson, C.B. *et al.* (1981) *Understanding Psychology*, Weidenfeld and Nicolson, London.

Goffman, E. (1961), *Asylums*, Penguin, Harmondsworth.

Hollingworth, S. (1985) *Preparation for Change: Preparing Nurse Tutors in Initial Training for a Change to Nursing Process*, RCN, London.

Larson, E. *et al.* (1984) Job satisfaction: assumptions and complexities. *Journal of Nursing Administration*, **14**(1), 31–8.

Martin, J.P. (1984) *Hospitals in Trouble*, Blackwell, Oxford.

Menzies, I. (1960) *The Functioning of Social Systems as a Defence Against Anxiety: A Report on a Study of the Nursing Service of a General Hospital*, Tavistock, London.

Metcalfe, C. (1983) A study of change in the method of organising the delivery of nursing care in a ward of a maternity hospital, in J. Wilson-Barnett (ed.) *Nursing Research: Ten Studies in Patient Care*, Wiley, New York and London, pp. 119–40.

O'Connor, A.B. (1982) Staff development: the problems of motivation. *Journal of Continuing Education in Nursing*, **13**(2), March–April, 10–14.

Royal College of Nursing (1981) *Ward Standards – a Discussion Document*, RCN, London.

Schein, E.H. (1980) *Organisational Psychology*, Prentice-Hall, Englewood Cliffs, NJ.

Shainberg, D. (1983) *Healing in psychotherapy: the process of holistic change*, Gordon and Breach Science Publishers, London, p. 52.

Towell, D. (1975) *Understanding Psychiatric Nursing: A Sociological Analysis of Modern Psychiatric Nursing*, Royal College of Nursing, London.

Towell, D. and Harries, C. (1979) *Innovation in Patient Care*, Croom Helm, London.

United Kingdom Central Council for Nursing, Midwifery and Health Visiting (1984) *Care of Professional Conduct for Nurses, Midwives and Health Visitors*, UKCC, London.

Vernon, M.D. (1971) *The Psychology of Perception*, Penguin Books, Harmondsworth.

Ward, M.J. and Moran, S.J. (1984) Resistance to change: recognise, respond, overcome. *Nursing Management*, **15**(1), January, 30–3.

Wright, D. (1984) An introduction to the evaluation of nursing care: a review of the literature. *Journal of Advanced Nursing*, **9**, 457–67.

Zaltman, G. and Duncan, R. (1977) *Strategies for Planned Change*, John Wiley, New York, p. 63.

— 4 —
Groupwork as the focus

> Among the ordinary English. . .the habit of not speaking to others, nor much even to themselves, about the things in which they do feel interest, causes both their feelings and their intellectual faculties to remain undeveloped, reducing them, considered as spiritual beings, to a kind of negative existence. (J.S. Mill)

John Stuart Mill's observation here may seem unfair. After all, people of any culture – ordinary or not – may not consider an expression of personal feelings to be quite their cup of tea. Still, the tradition of individual work was strong in the British education system, compared to schooling in the USA, for example. How amenable we are to sharing our view in groups at work may say something about past experience. A more familiar addage (but perhaps no less unfair) is 'Nurses think with their feet'. Although you may not think a statement like that is true today, we have attempted to show in Chapter 1 how aspects of our past get transferred to the here and now. In this chapter we try to show how the past and present actually come to the fore, in a useful way, in groups. This will involve practical examples of ward team staff support groups, sisters' groups, and quality circles, for example. First, for readers not familiar with the group process, let us explore groupwork, with a view to its usefulness in managing change, for instance, a change in attitude from task- to client-centred care.

4.1 INTRODUCTION

We live in groups. Our private thoughts involve other people. And even our dreams may include other people. We seem to thrive in groups, such as the family; yet the group can, in certain situations, become an enraged mob, having little in common with the intentions of its individual members. While in this chapter we present the group as a means to learning and questioning at work, comparisons are also made with other kinds of group, whether a picnic with friends or a staff meeting.

Part of the joint experience that is presented in this book is that we derived from the Cassel Hospital, a psychotherapeutic community located near Richmond, Surrey. Here families and individuals are helped through emotional distress without the use of tranquillizers, or exposure to insects (for those people who have phobias to insects), with groupwork used as a method for finding answers to questions, and for learning and teaching. Both the staff, nurses and doctors, and clients are involved in group processes, the largest of which is the hospital-as-a-community group.

Before the Management of Change Project started, an evaluation was made of the nursing assistants' (NAs') training (see Chapter 3). Although the nursing assistants' course became increasingly related to ward-based happenings, it became clear that other members of the ward team had to be involved in their learning in order for clients to benefit from their teaching. In Chapter 2 we have related the educational relevance of experiential learning to psychiatric nursing, in so far as the personal qualities required of the nursing mean that learning requires personal growth for nurse and client. Groupwork supports this thesis.

It we look at each of the groups in the Management of Change Project, in order from first to last, we can illustrate how they can be used in teaching and research. We then look at some of the patterns which the groups have in common as an introduction to the theory of group dynamics. Here is a list of the groups:

1. The Nursing Assistant Training Course, during 1983;
2. The Nursing Assistant Monitoring Group, during 1983–4;
   (a) what did we want to find out?
   (b) what are the learning difficulties?
3. Ward Team Staff Support Groups, 1984–6;
4. The Management of Change Project Steering Group, 1984–6;
5. Sisters' Group, 1985–6;
6. Quality Circles, 1986.

Between 1975 and 1982 the Nursing Assistant Monitoring Group had run enough two-week and one-week follow-up courses to enable most of the 150 nursing assistants to attend. These courses were conducted by a ward sister, who acted as a training officer; when the sister's post became vacant, the Monitoring Group decided to employ a nursing officer, whose first task would be to evaluate the training to date. The evaluation which followed, during 1983, revealed to the Monitoring Group the need for a different approach to training. This was a group representing the personnel department, nursing management, and the education department at the mental hospital in Tooting Bec. In Fig. 4.1 the kind of nursing school-based course which had been running, albeit updated from the pre-1980 time-table for nursing assistants is illustrated. Figure 4.2 illustrates how the course began to change, involving training staff in and out of school and reflecting early evaluation findings. The Monitoring Group was in fact disbanded in 1984, after the nursing assistant training was suspended. Not only had most NAs been to the course, but the evaluation identified that learning difficulties were due to the need for post-basic training and education. Because of the focus upon trained staff, the nursing officer for in-service training was transferred to the Staff Development Department of the Nightingale School of Nursing (West Lambeth Health Authority), with responsibility for the Management of Change Project. Members of the disbanded Monitoring Group, with the exception of the member from the personnel department, became part of the new Project Steering Group. The evaluation of the NAs' course pointed to the conclusion that nursing assistants, or any members of a ward team, could not use their training if the trained staff were not prepared to practise at a similar standard of nursing to that which was taught. The Monitoring Group, and after it the Project Steering Group, were committed to addressing the age-old problem of the 'hidden curriculum', that what is taught in the psychiatry school is not practised on the ward. The Steering Group operated along the lines of a committee, with an appointed leader and secretary, for instance, from among its members. These groups each had their terms of reference, so that members knew the rules and the aims, objectives, and minutes of the tasks at hand. In Fig. 4.3 a–c the framework of these groups is shown, using the Management of Change Steering Group's terms of reference as an example.

In contrast to these two groups, the rules and conduct of the Ward Team Staff Support Groups, the Sisters' Group, and the Quality Circles would be determined by their participants; these three will

	MONDAY	TUESDAY	WEDNESDAY	THURSDAY	FRIDAY
8.45 am	Course administration Interpersonal communication and interaction	Mental health legislation St Thomas' Health Authority	Assisting with drug round Helping with electro-convulsive therapy	9 00 am – 12 00 pm Care of the elderly ↓	Psychiatric first aid
10.30 am	Admission/ Discharge/ Transfer/ Death/ Nursing procedures	10 00 am – 12 30 pm Practical ward experience Visit to ↓	Reality orientation technique ↓	Physical illness	Crisis intervention
11.30 am	The law and the nurse (Elementary)	admission and rehabilitation wards	Practice	At St Thomas' Hospital wards ↓	Video/discussion
1.30 pm	Care of property and valuables	Occupational therapy on the ward	Attachment to day centre and/or ↓	Care of the elderly	Your views and suggestions
2.30 pm	Basic ward routine s and management	Social therapy off the ward	Home Help services 1 30 – 5 30 pm	Mentally ill Beechlawn Day Centre Tooting Bec Hospital	End of course discussion with
3.30 pm	Preparation for 'visits'			2 00 pm – 4 00 pm	Ward Nurses

Fig. 4.1 This time-table illustrates the focus for training before The Management of Change Project. In contrast to Fig. 4.2, the subjects below stress procedure, custody and illness.

	MONDAY	TUESDAY	WEDNESDAY	THURSDAY	FRIDAY
8.45 am	Welcome Introductions Unique role of nursing assistants	What's in a locker Dignity/privacy Property/activity independence (ward-based)	The ins and outs of body heat Focus on eating	Emotional complications of mental illness: Skills to prevent anxiety	Ethics in nursing hospital etiquette Responsibility (Nursing officer)
10.30 am	Identify problems Aim to look at possible solutions	Approaches to the patient Language Tones, Aggression	Causes of pressure sores Focus on incontinence (ward-based)	Basic personal care Hygiene of skin, mouth feet, nails, hair Individuality (Sister)	How and where to get basic facts about nursing
11.30 am	Development of two case histories	Witnessing the medicine round Giving drugs (Sister)	Reporting: observations, accidents, changes in conditions and behaviour	Rest, sleep, mobility, body discharges, dress	Appraisal and retrospective view of Monday's problems
1.30 pm	Reality orientation Slide show 1 Discussion	Body language Postural echoing Video programme	The human body: design and load-bearing capacity	Social orientation Focus on tilted chairs Muscle tone/exercise (ward-based)	Pleasures and values in sharing, progressing the work
2.30 pm	Reality orientation Slide show 2 Discussion	Film on talking with the elderly	Opportunities for touching The meaning of words	Reminiscence and recall therapy Video/slide show Basic care	Evaluation with ward sisters, charge nurses, nursing officers, teachers
3.30 pm	Recap of the day Practice nursing	Recap with focus nursing process	Recap and practice	Recap and practice	Goodbye Home

Fig. 4.2 This time-table illustrates the focus for training during the project's first phase. This time-table illustrates a changing focus, to processes rather than tasks. to valuing the experience of learners, to participation of ward staff.

<u>A synopsis of the problem</u>

A programme designed for untrained staff attempted to use the expertize of professional staff. This led to the identification of knowledge and skills deficits in the latter group, which is likely to compromize acceptable standards of care.

<u>A suggested solution (2 year plan)</u>

Aim:

To ensure that the staff involved in the five wards are self-supporting in a problem-solving approach to care (Fig 4.3c is a process illustration) and are able and willing to monitor their own standards of care.

Objectives:

1 Provide safe, effective, satisfying nursing care;

2 Make opportunities to promote personal and professional growth for providers of care;

3 For nursing management, to support and help facilitate assessment, planning, implementation, and evaluation of nursing;

4 Develop standards of care;

5 Provide the basis for learning.

Action:

Short term (a) Continuing staff support groups
(b) Providing base-line quality appraisal with continued emphasis on action research;
(c) Disseminating information to staff re (b) above.

Middle term (a) Develop formal teaching sessions from group work;
(b) Enhance management skills
- leadership
- conflict
- assertion.

Long term (a) Evaluate first year's work in August 1985;
(b) Plan future strategy in view of this diagnosis;
(c) Plan conclusion

Fig. 4.3a Terms of reference for the Management of Change Project Steering Group.

Weekly Ward Team Meetings February - July 1985

CHANGE AND THE MANAGEMENT OF CHANGE IN FIVE WARDS

The Group Facilitators: Kathleen McClafferty, Liz Carter, Geoff Haines, Bill Lemmer

Focus of the work;

Use problem-solving approach; look at attitudes and needs.

Aims:

1 To recognize patients and staff as individuals with specific needs; provide support to meet these needs;

2 To foster effective communication and teamwork;

3 To identify roles and responsibilities;

4 To provide a nursing base which can be developed.

Objectives:

1 Attending, with a senior nurse, ward team reports and subsequent nursing discussion of specific issues in patient care (1 30 - 2 30 pm);

2 Assisting staff to identify an area of care to be developed in the ward and setting weekly goals;

3 Assessing development; providing feedback on progress through weekly meetings;

4 Providing ward-based teaching, toward meeting identified needs;

5 Monitoring and recording, as participant observers, the process of nursing; evaluating the work with other facilitators, key people, and the ward team;

6 Recommending appropriate staff development activity;

7 Discussing staff roles and responsibilities in light of United Kingdom Central Council (UKCC) Code of Conduct and district policies.

Fig. 4.3b Terms of reference for Ward Team Staff Support Group.

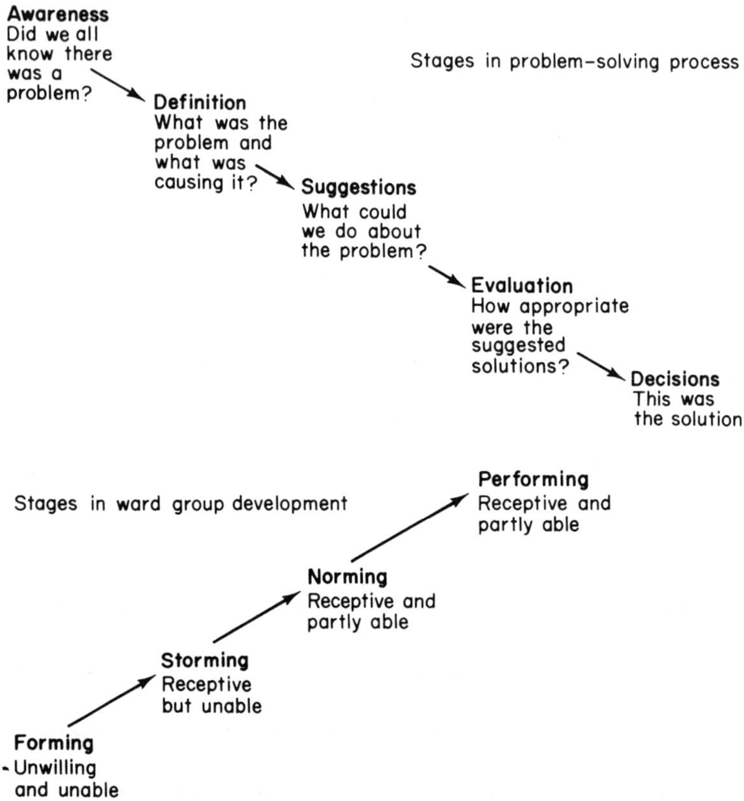

Fig. 4.3c A process illustration of a team approach to care, *Nursing Times*, Dec. 12th 1984, pp. 50–51.

be the focus of this chapter. The questions we address here are: do these small groups enable people to interact more effectively with others in such a way as to foster attitudes of patient-centred nursing? Do such groups provide a method of learning how to improve standards of care? What is the effect of using a group as a research method?

4.2 WARD TEAM STAFF SUPPORT GROUPS

The principal idea in groupwork throughout the Management of Change Project is to pay more attention to individuals, and to value people regardless of their grade or status in the organization. After all, how can you expect individualized care to be delivered to patients if it is not delivered also to the staff? The groupwork aims to present a model of care which, in itself, teaches person-centred care, communication skills, and colleagueship; that is, the way a group works presents a model of how nursing can be approached, for example, by sharing and using the views of others, concentrating on people's individuality, and by valuing individuals who are, or have been, devalued by virtue of their working or living in mental hospital.

In all, there were 25 meetings for each ward team, once a week, with a teacher-facilitator for each ward team group and a senior nurse member who would be the manager of the ward, or in his/her absence another senior nurse. Because of the off-duty rota, holidays, and absence due to sickness, these were small groups with about five nurses present each week, i.e. half of the ward team. On occasions, eight members of the team were present, with the senior nurse and facilitator making a group of ten.

The fundamental nature of a group lies in its experience; it is learning by experience. The group is a way of teaching group processes, i.e. by using the actual group of learners as a model of group behaviour. This has been called 'gut learning' because it is concerned with expanding conscious experience in structured and controlled situations (Douglas, 1976). What happens in the group can be understood, in part, by considering what would happen if all groups were removed, leaving each of us as an individual alone. There is a seeking to belong in groups, to be sociable, to be willing to allow the group to function. To a certain extent, members of groups give at least temporary lip-service to judgement of other members with whom they do not really or completely agree. The way this working acceptance occurs is what distinguishes how we are in groups. This happens to each individual in a process which enables each person to learn more about him or herself. It is this aspect of learning about ourselves which seems to us important when we are considering attitude change as a part of the development to individualized care in the hospital. Douglas, in the first of his two basic books about groupwork listed eight assumptions upon which group practice is founded (Douglas, 1976, pp. 28–9):

1. Group experience is universal and an essential part of human existence;

2. Groups can be used to effect changes in the attitudes and behaviour of individuals;
3. Groups provide experiences which can be monitored or selected in some way for beneficial ends – life outside the group is in no way neglected; it tends to be 'put out of focus' in favour of considering the here and now situation within the group;
4. Groups offer experience shared with others, so that all can come to have something in common with the sense of belonging and of growing together;
5. Groups produce change which is more permanent than can be achieved by other methods and change which is obtained more quickly also;
6. Groups assist in the removal or diminution of difficulties created by previous exposure to the process of learning;
7. Groups as instruments of helping others may be economical in the use of scarce resources, e.g. skilled workers, time, etc.;
8. Groups can examine their own behaviour, and in so doing, learn about the general patterns of group behaviour (process).

Therefore, two aspects of learning that we seek in the group process are cohesiveness and interpersonal learning. Here one of the fundamental ideas to bear in mind is that the groupwork brings to mind and gives expression to feelings that have not previously been expressed – as these emotions and desires are expressed there is an experience of relief and sometimes the restoring of composure in such a way as to enable growth and personal development to continue. These are the kinds of change, then, including the change in attitude which can be reflected in a care plan and to which we have already referred in Chapter 2, which we consider as being important to nurse education in mental health care.

The five ward team groups were begun early in 1985. Bill Lemmer, who was by then a teacher in the Staff Development Department (Nightingale School) and began the Management of Change Project from its NA course origins and co-ordinated it, acted as the facilitator for three wards. Liz Carter, Nursing Process Coordinator for West Lambeth Health Authority, was the facilitator for a fourth elderly care ward, and another staff development teacher, Geoff Haines was the third facilitator. Kathleen McClafferty, senior nurse in the elderly care area of the hospital and Bill's partner in the NA course development and Management of Change Project, was back-up facilitator for all five wards with the responsibility for liaison with the senior nurse group in the hospital. These four people met every two weeks as an unstructured group to share and discuss their roles in the ward team meetings. This sharing in a group by facilitators, without a leader and with no minutes, was to provide a support and monitoring function. Each of the ward team staff support groups would be written up by the facilitator in a diary; this report of the groups was kept at the Education Department, but available to be seen. In other words, the reporting by facilitators was a collection of data, using the participant observation method; and an analysis of the content of these reports of groups could be made by a practitioner, in addition to the Management of Change Steering Group. In this chapter we offer a selection of this data from facilitators.

During the four months up to 1985, there was a series of feedback meetings. This process involved reporting the findings of the NA course evaluation to the NAs, the senior nurse group in the hospital, the ward sisters of the five wards, and the enrolled nurses. The major findings of the evaluation were validated by these participants, e.g. that ward managers did not have the authority required to manage change and that school-based teaching had not been implemented in the practice setting of the ward.

Instances of conversations or incidents which reflected the five categories were made in the content analysis of three of the wards; these categories and the number of instances are noted below and are followed by examples:

Categories	*Ward 1*	*Ward 2*	*Ward 3*
Attitudes	26	36	45
Patient problems	13	20	19
Role	12	18	10
Structure	13	21	18
Conflict between day and night nursing	0	2	13
	64	97	105 = 266

The numbers are not all that relevant, because they do not allow us to generalize or predict anything. However, the lower number of instances on Ward 1, compared to Ward 3, would appear to confirm the Management of Change Steering Group's original judgement that ward 1 was in a better position to express positive attitudes than Ward 3. At the outset, two of the five wards in the project were thought by the Steering Group to have a better standard of care than two other wards in the project. However, the two better wards, as they were originally perceived, had less of a focus upon patient problems, as would seem to be reflected in the numbers shown above. Furthermore, the facilitators judged that Ward 2, which was not a 'better ward', was more successful than Ward 1 during the groupwork at addressing patients' problems. The effect of this success upon attitudes is reflected in the ward's change in emphasis from custodial to individualized care.

The following instances are taken from the Ward 1 facilitator's report and are instances judged to characterize 'attitudes':

(March) 'The patients played up today.' 'She's going down.'

(April) 'The night staff routine doesn't fit into the transition to individualized care.'

(May) 'Where do critical incidents go?'

(June) 'The lady who shouts and hits out at the nurses, none of her daily baths or application of lotions are written in the care plan.' (comment by facilitator)

'Mobility/exercise (in the patient care plan under "Action") – refer to physiotherapist.'

'Authority is in each person.' (sister's comment)

'It's worse being battered by your organization than hit by a patient because you can learn to live with the patient.'

(July) 'There is little talking-across behaviour in subgroups, compared to the March–June period.' (facilitator)

The following comments are from the content analysis of the facilitators' diary (Ward 1), characterizing 'role':

(March) 'Nurses should not have to lift patients.'

'Doctors are used to solve nursing problems.' (facilitator)

(May) 'The senior nurse is in and out of the group, attending to one thing and then another.' (facilitator)

(June) 'There is a dispute between sister and an NA – the team

allows that both views are equally valid.' (facilitator)
'We are being blocked in trying to give individual care by higher authority.'

Comments from Ward 2 were judged by the facilitator to characterize 'attitudes':

(March) 'These patients are going down. . . what else can you say? People can't see the problem.'
(April) 'Psychological care isn't possible under the pressure of tasks.'
'Individual patients' problems are mentioned during report.' (facilitator)
(May) 'Team resolved its disagreements regarding named nurses would look after a group of patients.' (facilitator)
'Each shift of nurses is planning the care of 12 patients.'
(June) 'The patient group and the staff group seem calmer. . . staff decide to review a care plan.' (facilitator)
(July) 'Well, you just can't do any more with these people.'
'Nurses have progressed on problem-solving and accountability.' (facilitator)

The following comments from Ward 2 characterized views about role:

(March) 'You [i.e. facilitator] tell us what do you want us to do?'
'Shifting conflicts within the group.' (facilitator)
(April) 'There is a lack of co-operation with night staff.'
(May) 'The facilitator said he was not the group's leader.'

Ward 2 had the highest number of instances of terms used under the category 'patients' problems'. Despite a lower perceived standing in the hospital (both in terms of nursing care standards and morale), compared to the highest in Ward 1 before 1985, Ward 2 showed the most interest in direct patient care; and its combined score (54) for instances of comment characterizing 'attitudes' and 'roles' was higher than Ward 1's (38). Ward 2 expressed higher scores in the content analysis in every category than Ward 1, whose overall content analysis score was 69, compared to Ward 1's 97.

Ward 2's use of groupwork suggests on the evidence of this analysis that its position in comparison with Ward 1 is reversed after the six-month period as a result of the ward team's ability to redirect attention to patient-focused issues, whereas Ward 1, confident in their use of the nursing process, appeared to indicate that individual patients' nursing plans were not as important an issue in care as what impinged upon care from outside the ward team.

Ward 3 experienced the highest rate of sister absence (37%) during the six months. It demonstrated both the highest overall content analysis score (105), the largest amount of discussion focusing upon 'attitudes' and 'role', and the single highest score of the three wards in the 'attitudes' category (45). They also reported the highest number of reported conflicts with night staff (13), compared with the unsolicited instances counted from the facilitators' diary of the other two wards.

The following are instances characterizing 'attitudes' from Ward 3:

(February) 'Nurses late.' 'Sister wants to leave early.' (facilitator)
'There's nothing you can do with these patients.'
'They're all [the patients] going down hill.'

(March) 'Patients described in subjective terms, e.g. noisy, incontinent plus shouting.' (facilitator)
'Nurses' conflicts with patients are discussed by visitors at the 49 bus stop.'
'Visitor not welcomed to the ward.'

(April) 'Late start.' (facilitator)
'The nurse–patient allocation (one nurse accounts for care of a group of patients) is not working.'
'These patients' problems are much the same.'

(May) 'Late start.' (facilitator) 'Nursing goals are ignored.' (facilitator) 'The group seems to lack a shared purpose.' 'Two patients put forward for care planning.' (facilitator)

(June) 'Nurses late.' (facilitator) 'Sister wants to leave early.'

(July) 'Imaginative plan to motivate patients, using social centre.' (facilitator)

Instances characterizing views about 'role' from Ward 3 diary included:

(February) 'Visitor favours one sister; uncertainty in team.' (facilitator)

(March) 'Three patients claim to be next of kin of one patient but they are not – the patient's personal documents disappear and the visitors complain.' (facilitator)

'Individual care prescribed is not carried out by others, day and night.'

(April) 'Nurses cannot lift a lady, but the physio can.'

(May) 'There is a question about NAs going to other wards to give drugs.' (facilitator)

'Conflict about the conduct of the group meeting.' (facilitator)

'The ward manager (sister) is not taking a full role in practical nursing.'

'A visitor refuses to respect the patients' privacy – a man who just troops into the dormitory.'

The sickness absence rate increased by 65% for Ward 1, compared with the same six-month period in 1984, and it increased by 59.5% for Ward 3, but decreased by 49% for Ward 2. Overall, the five wards showed an average improvement during the groupwork of 9% – lowering the number of days lost in the first six months of 1984 from 709 to 644 during the first half of 1985. The Ward 1 and Ward 3 figures are distorted by 144 instances of sister sickness/absence. There was no ward establishment in the elderly care area at this time, and measures to control nursing levels were variable and inconsistent.

The confidentiality of these ward team staff support groups prevents a more exacting report here of conversations, for example, which would illustrate the process of how individuality in patient care became more of an issue as time went on in the 1985 groups. Evidence of personal and interpersonal growth in the groupwork is also apparent in the six-month process which is detailed in the facilitators' diary. Extracts from Wards 4 and 5 may provide more of a picture than the content analysis of the direction of the group process.

Ward 4: 'The organization of the first few meetings was slightly confused. The main problems revolved around finding a quiet place to meet, so we could hear each other speak, getting where possible a nurse from another ward to be with the patients and reaching agreement on what time the meeting should start and finish. These difficulties were to a greater extent resolved.'

'The content of the groups often revolved around the themes of low staffing levels, which patients it was appropriate to use incontinence aids on, the booking out of staff, the requisitioning of occupational therapy equipment for the ward not being followed up, the difficulties in implementing more individualized forms of care, the role of nursing assistants in writing care plans.'

'On some occasions we went on to discuss issues such as communication problems within the nursing hierarchy, relationship difficulties and misperceptions between different nurses and inconsistencies in styles of working between different shifts.'

'Most meetings with the nurses began with them asking me to open the discussion. Eventually, however, their level of dependency appeared to decrease, and although they would at first expect me to begin the group, they would quickly take over.'

'Towards the end of my time facilitating the group I told the staff that I believed we had not made the group safe enough to talk openly about the staff relationship problems that I was told about outside the group. Following this, we did discuss these issues in greater depth.'

Ward 5: 'Initial meetings established the nature of the work and the role of the facilitator. Throughout the six months it was evident that both of these concepts proved hard for the staff to grasp. Set routines had been established which, being familiar, were safer for the staff to follow. The ward meetings provided the opportunity for staff to voice their opinions and make decisions concerning aspects of care – something which they had not experienced before.'

'Patient allocations had just been introduced at the beginning of the February to July 1985 work. Nurses showed considerable interest in their own patients, and more detailed knowledge of the patients' abilities, rather than problems, emerged. Greater attention was paid to the details of care. Four patients were moved into ordinary chairs and integrated more into the life of the ward. One of the ladies was subsequently able to walk, much to the amazement of the staff.'

'With these changes in care, the focus of responsibility also changed – the nurse in charge of a group of patients sharing decision-making with the Sister. The burden of this was evident when one patient suffered a fracture. Criticism was levelled at the staff from several different quarters and they felt very alone. The deficiencies in the support structure for nurses at ward level was highlighted. Following this incident, a more concerted effort was made, at Senior Nurse and Sister level, to support junior staff.'

'Commitment to the work varied during the course of the six months. It is notable that the meetings where both a Sister and Senior Nurse were in attendance, more was achieved. Decisions could be made under guidance, but more work needs to be done on this as there is a tendency to tell staff what to do, or do it for them, rather than explore options.'

'There was a readiness on the part of staff to discuss the social and family backgrounds of the patients, which was relevant to their care. The concern of some members of staff was good to see.'

'Physical illness amongst the patients occurred on several occasions, ranging from chest infections, leg ulcers, pressure sores to fractures. The knowledge deficit in this area was quite considerable, and even after six months remains a problem. Uncertainty about appropriate action to take and delay in implementing the action (often caused by waiting for a doctor or someone else to assume responsibility) were both features of this.'

'The ward environment was drab as it needed redecoration. With encouragement the staff put up new pictures and re-arranged some of the furniture. Although there is a lot still to be achieved, a start has been made.'

'Towards the end of the six months there was stronger evidence of teamwork amongst the nurses and also a greater degree of safety within the group. Individuals were able to discuss how they felt when a patient was aggressive towards them, and how they handled the situation. Some of the nurses were very creative and sensitive in their approach, while others resorted to old coping mechanisms – handling patients roughly, shouting at them and confining them to Buxton chairs. The thinking and the attitudes of some of the staff has not changed. At handover report they frequently talk all at once, and need to be reminded to listen to each other.'

'During the six months several patients were transferred out to other wards. Staff noticed that in some activities they had become more dependent, where previously they were independent. Through discussion they began to show signs of identifying what was an acceptable standard of care, and the importance of continuity of care.'

Using groupwork as a method in action research may well employ the highest level of reality of any investigative process. Feedback between participants, including the groups' facilitators, also provides a realistic check against what is being recorded in the diary. At the same time, groupwork as a research method may provide the least amount of control and precision, compared to conventional forms of enquiry. Some of the differences between our approach to research and teaching and traditional approaches can be seen in the following list of forms of enquiry, from Guba (1978), in Gilbert and Pope, 1987, p. 49):

Points of comparison	*Conventional enquiry*	*Naturalistic enquiry*
Purpose	To verify	To discover
Conditions	Controlled	Open to interference
Setting	Laboratory	In relevant, natural context
Style	Intervention	Selection
Treatment	Stable	Varies

These points of comparison are useful because they illustrate why groupwork as a research method is not intended either to predict outcomes or generalize our findings and apply them elsewhere. The facilitators are teachers who are doing research as a part of their teaching. The diary is a way of monitoring which enables the facilitators to analyse how the teaching–learning situation in the group is developing. The groups make suggestions and the action research thrust of interchange and feedback lead to new approaches being tried out, with the impact on the teaching and learning monitored in the group and outside. By outside, we refer both to the diary and the regular meeting of (a) facilitators themselves, and (b) facilitators as members of the Project Steering Group. The outcome of this process is intended to expand the practitioners' knowledge of the phenomena that he/she is dealing with rather than provide generalizable statements. So a point of further comparison may be that conventional enquiry may be reductionist whereas a naturalistic enquiry may be expansionist. What distinguishes action research from traditional research (based upon experimentation and control of variables) is therefore not only the process and methods of enquiry, but also what one does with the findings (i.e. one does not make general assumptions and inferences from them). Therefore, the comments and summaries, of the ward team staff support groups, above, do illustrate how groups can be used both for interpersonal and intrapersonal gain, in the aid of improving patient care. As researchers, we look at the facilitators' data, in the diary, for indications of change, for example, in attitudes and skills that address patient-centred problems rather than task-centred problems. If the Management of Change Project had been approached as a conventional enquiry, we would have examined facts and their relationship to one another. However, we chose an approach concerned with describing and understanding social phenomena in such a way as people involved in the project could learn from the process of enquiry.

4.3 SISTERS' GROUP (1985–6)

The Sisters' Group was begun in November 1985. Between July and November each of the facilitators was involved in monthly follow-up ward team staff support groups and the data from the six months' work was being evaluated. Throughout 1985, and continuing through 1986, the Staff Development Department provided study days and workshops which supported the Management of Change Project. For example, study days about care planning and assertion skills were provided along with workshops on team-building. The 25 weekly Sisters' Groups would be facilitated by Bill Lemmer and Kathleen McClafferty.

Kathleen and Bill had been working with the other facilitators to an agreed, although not highly specified, formula about the ward team staff support groups. They would receive all communications from their groups. Their responses would be non-directive, although they would clarify and, to a limited extent, interpret events within the group. For example, the relationship which a member of a group forms with facilitator is made the object of communication and of analysis. This interpretation would occur only in relation to the activities of living for patients on the ward. For instance, the common relationship made with the facilitator by a group – in the early stages of their six months more so than at the end – would be symbolized by the expression, 'Well, what do you want us to do, then?' The individual facilitator would then have to decide (a) how to be non-directive in his/her response, and (b) how to address the issue of the inherent value and authority of the group and its members. One facilitator might decide to say: 'I have no power here to provide direction for you; that (he/she would stress, to clarify his/her role) would come from within yourselves.' Another facilitator might ask a question about the dependency of the patients, or of a particular individual. A lady who was striking out at the nurses in one ward, for example, was the source of much anxiety by the nurses. Enabling the team to develop a plan of care which would manage and alleviate their stress and reduce the hitting out was a facilitator's way of teaching nurses about their own values and skills coming from within rather than from without. Remember that this Project is about research and teaching which selects and expands rather than intervenes and reduces by controlled experiment. We learned from the Ward Team Staff Support Groups that ward sisters wanted to exercise leadership and recognized that they must do that if the process and standard of nursing was to improve. Sisters were usually nominated as leaders during the course of a ward team meeting; but this occurred in such a needy and demanding way that facilitators wished to share their own skills with the sisters in a separate learning group. At the same time, further study days and workshops would be provided for sisters. The evidence of the Ward Team Staff Support Groups was that the nursing management system at that time prevented sisters from exercising authority and control; additionally, there was a deficit in nursing skills and ward management to be addressed. Therefore, a Sisters' Group would be necessary, if as planned, the ward teams could be self-sufficient when the Management of Change Project finished in late 1986.

Before leaving the discussion of the facilitators' attitude in groupwork, let us illustrate from Douglas (1976, p. 14) the basic orientation we followed by first showing a range of choices:

Theoretical backgrounds	*Structure analysis of variables*	*Variables which influence interaction*
Field theory	Group attractiveness	The qualities of the group
Interaction theory	Interaction of	Group goal(s)
Systems theory	Role dynamics	The qualities of the task
Sociometric theory	Sociometric choice	The qualities of the task
Psychoanalytic theory	Norms	The qualities of members
General psychology		The qualities of members
Empiricist statistical theory		External relationships
Formal model theory	Power relationships	

Our orientation is in the areas of field theory, general psychology, and interaction. As such, facilitators are not inclined to interpret the relationship of two people in a group. A common feature of early Ward Team Staff Support Groups was the development of subgroups, in twos and threes, which eventually disrupted the whole group. In allowing the chaos, facilitators usually would clarify for the group the equal value of all members by asking the group if it wished to hear from the subgroups. Frequently the nursing assistants would repeat to the whole group a useful and relevant point which derived from their experience in the patients' care. The disciplined attitude of facilitators towards the value of equal participation was paramount, while the passing of attitudes from one person to another was not neglected. People had to account for what they said, particularly when this occurred in a subgroup or was coloured in the process of transferring it to another person. As with the Ward Team Staff Support Groups, the Sisters' Group was not prepared by the Management of Change Project to explore the development of attitudes, positive or negative, towards the facilitator or anyone else. Our attitude work with the nurses was in relation to their nursing, and in this sense transference was to a limited extent addressed by facilitators.

The learning of these groups (the Ward Team Staff Support Groups, the Sisters' Group, and Quality Circles), and the nature of change in groupwork, is referred to by Blumberg and Golembiewski (1976, p. 142) as dealing singly or in combination with the following:

> Attitudes or values, which define persons, objects, or opinions as variously desirable, preferable, or acceptable;
> Emotions or affective states of the individuals involved;
> Perceptual skills, which involve developing greater competence in observing what is happening in personal and group contacts, as well as gaining greater confidence in sensing and feeling;
> Cognitive knowledge or intellectual understanding of recurring patterns in human relationships, which is typically reflected in an increasingly useful and complete model of reality;
> Behavioural skills, which involve acting on the environment to increase the probability that desired consequences occur.

Learning and change are measured by real advances in the individualization of patient care, compared to the nursing assistant course evaluation data, and nurses' perceptions of reality that would substantiate improved standards of care (Blumberg and Golembiewski, 1976, p. 152):

work as more human and less impersonal;
clear connections between the meeting of interpersonal needs and effectiveness at work;
personal needs as a more significant part of problems at work;
less need to lay responsibility on others for problems at work.

The outcomes that result from these interpersonal and intergroup processes are expressed in the way that organization and delivery of care expand the activities of daily living in which the patients are engaged.

The Sisters' Group followed patterns we observed in the five Ward Team Staff Support Groups. All of the groups experienced a period of orientation which had similar features. Two examples are (a) wanting to know what to do and (b) looking outward and inward at the same time. As far as the second of these is concerned, what was most valued came from participants and not facilitators providing answers to the question 'what do we do?' Also, there was a constant balancing between self-consciousness and focusing on something outside of self-awareness. An example of this latter pattern is that group members easily concentrated on a problem away from themselves, such as staff shortages — when a colleague changed the focus of attention to the number of leg ulcer patients on the ward, for instance; there appeared in the expression of the staff-shortage advocate an inward-looking self-awareness. It was as if the person who presented the staff-shortage point was not received as she had intended to be and was reflecting about herself rather than pushing the point. This self-consciousness arises from feedback and is a feature of social integration. Our group process was similar to Tuckman's (1965) findings, based upon a number of groups, which suggested that there are four main phases, and that both group structure and task activity develop in parallel ways (Argyle, 1969, p. 218), as shown on p. 75.

A district nurse researcher's post had been created by the chief nursing officer. This post was held by Martin Smits. He joined the four facilitators of Ward Team Staff Support Groups to review a number of evaluation tools; these are described in Chapters 8 and 9. But for the Sisters' Group, we decided to modify slightly the

	Group structure	*Task activity*
1. *Forming*	There is anxiety, dependence on a leader, testing to find out situation and what behaviour is acceptable	Members find out what the task is, what the rules are, and what methods are appropriate
2. *Storming*	Conflict between subgroups, rebellion against leader, opinions are polarized, resistance to control by group conflicts over intimacy	Emotional resistance to demands of task
3. *Norming*	Development of group cohesion, norms emerge, resistance overcome and conflicts patched up, mutual support, and development of group feeling	Open exchange of views and feeling: co-operation develops
4. *Performing*	Interpersonal problems are resolved, interpersonal structure is the tool of task activity, roles are flexible and functional	Emergence of solutions to problems, constructive attempts at task completion, energy is now available for effective work in major work period

Therapeutic Nursing Function (TNF) Indicator (Kitson, 1986) (see Appendix A to this chapter). This was given to each of the ten sisters at the beginning of the Sisters' Group and at the end of the groupwork. The TNF Indicator is designed to give a score for a therapeutic sister. However, as we in the Management of Change Project were concerned in the main with those values which come from within nurses, we focused upon the expansion of attitudes and skills expressed in the second TNF, as compared to the first. The scores for the questionnaire were too low to meet the sisters' needs for development and growth, and so we did not use the scores but referred to the TNF Indicator content changes. Also this was more in keeping with our research style.

4.4 QUALITY CIRCLES (1985–6)

The Quality Circles ran alongside the Sisters' Group, between November 1985 and May 1986, with the Sisters' Group alternating every other week with the Quality Circle on each of the five wards. A Quality Circle is a small group of employees who meet regularly to identify, analyse, and solve problems related to their work. There was a series of 12-hour-long circles, once a fortnight. They were facilitated by a senior nurse who had no direct, ongoing management responsibility for the ward. This senior nurse was Kathleen McClafferty. She co-ordinated this work, and a self-monitoring tool (see Appendix A to this chapter). Our intention in the development of this group was to help managers and nurses take in and use the values of teaching and learning that were being fostered by the Management of Change Project.

Notes were prepared to assist circle leaders, the senior nurse managers. Although the circles should be leader-centred, the basic idea of these groups is that the person doing the job on the shop-floor is an expert. The circles used a problem-solving process which consists of:

1. *Brainstorming*. This involves turn-taking by everyone (although anyone can 'pass'), recording of all ideas, even 'wild' ones, and evaluating the list;
2. *Selecting a problem*. This involves prioritizing the issues and setting about information-collecting;
3. *Possible causes*. This involves brainstorming causes to effects (examples of effects are:
   (a) an excessive interruption of an individual's care when members of the ward team are taken away to another ward in an unplanned way;
   (b) too many telephone calls at one particular time;
   (c) the lady who only wants to leave the ward but also needs help with an ulcer on her foot;
   (d) individuals who do not have access to their money;
   (e) the chairs people sit on are inappropriate;
   (f) too much time is spent on bathing in so far as the amount of time is not consistent with an individual's care plan goals;
   (g) a lack of communication regarding the disadvantages of a product, such as a continence aid, for a patient;

(h) patients' clothes being damaged or undignified; and
(i) the clinical room is dirty.) These effects, when identified, are monitored, and information about the monitoring is put on paper and recorded;

4. *Isolate most likely cause.* Possible causes might be related to manpower, resources, methods, and individuals' needs, for instance, and the causes would be lined up in a herring-bone diagram, with the effect at the head end and the causes along the body between the tail and the head;
5. *Determine the possible solutions.* This may take months, but thorough investigation is essential;
6. *Select a preferred solution.* Evaluate it, using the data;
7. *Arrange to present recommendations to implement the solution to management at the highest level appropriate,* e.g. a unit or district general manager or chairman of the health authority.

There were a number of problems identified by the circles and some progress was made in resolving them, for example, a recreational therapy annexe was improved. But there were many more problems that were not taken through the problem-solving process, such as: lack of privacy for patients as the result of not having curtains; broken bedpan washers; and acute shortages of laundry, including bed clothing and patients' clothing, of supplies including continence aids, and of staff. (Winston Churchill was quoted in a Quality Circle note, saying 'Give us the tools and we'll finish the job!') It was clear in reviewing the circles that leaders had not been sufficiently prepared for their role to facilitate the circles as leaders. Furthermore, the Quality Circles' records indicated that they focused upon tasks to such an extent that the processes involved were obscured. On the positive side, nurse managers were made keenly aware of the ward teams' ability on these five wards to assert and confidently defend the deficits in care for their patients. Other examples identified but not investigated for solution were unsatisfactory food, conflicts with visitors, leaders' absence, role conflict between sister and other nurses, a need for help in getting a lady back home in terms of getting the disciplines of medicine, social work, and nursing to work together, low morale, and patients being transferred to another ward without adequate information about their care, and restraint of restless patients.

4.5 CONCLUSION

The groupwork with Quality Circles made it clear that the ward teams had made significant changes individually and as groups, both in terms of cohesion and individual learning. However, in the process of bringing from outside the Management of Change Project values to use inside (as with the TNF Indicator and the Quality Circles' structure), it would appear that a great deal of care and preparation is needed if the outside values are to be consistent with the groupwork focus. On the positive side, there is evidence of real change in attitudes and interpersonal learning as measured in the outcome of care to patients. The groupwork itself is very time-consuming and requires special skills to facilitate. However, our argument would be that nursing in mental health care is about human qualities, and the evidence we have seen indicates that human services skills are already there. The groupwork in the Management of Change Project doesn't generalize elsewhere, but the reader will assess whether or not it might be a useful tool for teaching and researching in mental health care settings where change and standards of care are current issues. As a focus for learning, there is also a question of the utility of these groups during the transition to citizen-based mental health services.

REFERENCES

Argyle, M. (1969) *Social Interaction*, Tavistock, London.

Blumberg, A. and Golembiewski, R.T. (1976) *Learning and Change in Groups*, Penguin, Harmondsworth.

Douglas, T. (1976) *Groupwork Practice*, Tavistock, London.

Douglas, T. (1978) *Basic Groupwork*, Tavistock, London.

Foulkes, S.H. (1975) *Group-Analytic Psychotherapy: Methods and Principles*, Gordon and Breach, London.

Foulkes, S.H. and Anthony, E.J. (1965) *Group Psychotherapy: The Psychoanalytical Approach*, 2nd edn, Penguin, Harmondsworth.

Guba, E.G. (1978) Towards a methodology of naturalistic inquiry in educational evaluation, in J. Gilbert and M. Pope (eds) *Diploma in the Practice of Higher Education, Module J: Making Use of Research in Teaching and Learning* (*Extracts*, University of Surrey, Guildford, pp. 44–9).

Kitson, A.L. (1986) Indicators of quality in nursing care – an alternative approach. *Journal of Advanced Nursing*, **11**, 133–44.

9. Do you usually set time limits within which you can expect problems to be solved?

   always – noted in the Nursing Care Plan
   usually – written or expressed verbally
   sometimes – keep a mental note of the situation
   rarely – just don't know how things develop
   never

10. How do you monitor the progress of your patients' conditions in relation to their nursing needs?

11. How do staff on the ward obtain information regarding the day-to-day progress and care of their patients? (please tick)

    (a) daily nursing round with Sister
    (b) direct involvement in the planning and organizing of patient care by all grades of staff
    (c) reference to the nursing Kardex (individually reading and writing up of reports and care given)
    (d) reference to the nursing Kardex (collectively at report sessions in morning/afternoon/evening)
    (e) information communication of information between staff during work
    (f) reference to patient progress chart attached to nursing care plans
    (g) reference to information worksheets

Active management cycle

1. How do you inspect the daily needs of your patients? (please tick)

   (a) gather up information from various sources about each patient as best you can
   (b) make a point of seeing those patients who are ill and whose condition needs more careful consideration before delegating care
   (c) check on/monitor patients' conditions while performing other jobs, e.g. medicine rounds, rounds with the nursing officer or medical rounds
   (d) check on/monitor patients' progress while performing routine ward work with other members of staff
   (e) make a point of going round each patient every morning/coming on duty and discussing their condition with them
   (f) rely mainly on written reports and information from nursing staff during duty hours to monitor patients' needs.

2. Which of the following methods of prescribing nursing work is closest to the system used on this ward?

   (a) there is a system of ward task lists in the form of procedure books, ward lists, and duties for nurses
   (b) there is a set routine of work which everyone knows about
   (c) there is a Kardex sheet for each patient where instructions and comments are written in by ward sister and nurses caring for patients
   (d) there are individual worksheets for each patient, updated by ward sister each day which set out details of care for the patient

Tuckman, B.W. (1965) Developmental sequence in small groups. *Psychol. Bull.*, **63**, 384–99.

Yalom, I.D. (1975) *The Theory and Practice of Group Psychotherapy*, 2nd edn, Basic Books, New York.

APPENDIX A: THERAPEUTIC NURSING FUNCTION INDICATOR

Sisters' questionnaire (Tooting Bec Hospital)

INTRODUCTION

This questionnaire will be administered at the beginning and end of the Sisters' Group. It is intended to provide an evaluation of how beneficial this Sisters' Group has been.

Please complete the questionnaire and return it at the next Sisters' Group meeting. The questionnaire is totally confidential and will not be directly attributed to individuals.

Please follow the instructions for each question. Where a question asks you to tick, tick the appropriate number(s) or letter(s):

1 √   g √

SECTION 1: GOAL CONTENT

1. How would you describe nursing in your ward? (What does your nursing involve?)

2. Which of the following activities takes up most time on your ward? Please rank the activities listed below from 1–8 (1 being that activity which takes up most time and 8 that which takes up least of your time):

   (a) feeding patients, assisting patients with food
   (b) washing patients (not bathing)
   (c) caring for incontinent patients – washing, changing, cleaning
   (d) toileting, commoding, toilet training
   (e) dressing, undressing patients
   (f) caring for pressure areas
   (g) exercising immobile patients
   (h) communicating with patients

3. Many nurses working with the elderly have described their work as involving the following activities. Again, please rank activities in order of importance from 1 to 8:

   (a) carrying out medical treatment prescribed by the doctor
   (b) getting patients to move around and become more mobile
   (c) trying to teach and encourage patients to do things for themselves
   (d) keeping patients clean and comfortable
   (e) trying to create a relaxed atmosphere on the ward where patients feel 'at home'
   (f) caring for the physical needs of patients
   (g) stimulate patients to take an interest in surroundings and themselves
   (h) observing and recording medical progress of patients

SECTION 2: PRESCRIPTION/ORGANIZATION AND PLANNING OF NURSING CARE

Method of organizing work on the ward

1. What type of information do you make sure is collected from your patients to help assess and plan their nursing care?

2. How do you collect this information?

3. Who is responsible for collecting this information from the patients?

4. Now that this information is collected, where is it stored on the ward?

5. How do nurses working on the ward get access to this information?

6. What do you do with this information when it is collected?

7. Do you use structured Nursing Care Plans to organize care for each patient on your ward?

8. When you have identified the nursing problems of your patients do you:

   (a) inform your nursing staff and make a note of the problem(s) in the Kardex?
   (b) list the problems and offer nursing measures to cope with them?
   (c) make a written record of the problem on the Nursing Care Plan and offer nursing actions to solve them?
   (d) carry on with the ward routine (most patient problems can be dealt with in the daily routine of care)?
   (e) carry on with the ward work observing for changes in the patient's condition and noting any change?

(e) there is a nursing care plan for each patient setting out the details of care for the day

3. At the main report time of the day, where work is delegated to nurses, which of the following statements best describes the system of organizing work on this ward?

   (a) a report is given by ward sister to the trained staff on duty while the other nurses carry on with the routine ward work; after the report, the trained staff start the routine work along with the other nurses
   (b) a report is given by ward sister to all staff; team leaders are appointed and delegated to care for a number of patients; team leaders are responsible for the organizing of this work among their team members
   (c) ward sister and staff come together at the first opportunity and each patient's condition is discussed. The nursing workload is identified and nurses themselves decide who will perform each task
   (d) ward sister and staff come together at a prearranged time (usually the morning) for a report; each patient's nursing needs for the day are identified and each nurse is then given a plan of work to carry out for a group of patients
   (e) no regular morning report is given by ward sister; on most days ward work follows the well-known routine of the ward

4. There are *three* main ways of organizing work on the ward. Which is closest to your own system?

   (a) different nurses are organized to do just one particular job at a time for all patients on the ward
   (b) a group of nurses are allocated to one half of the ward and are responsible for the care of all patients in that area of the ward
   (c) nurses are given a group of patients to look after and do all the jobs for those patients
   (d) all three methods are used
   (e) don't know

5. Here are some methods used by nurses in reporting back on their work to the ward sister (please tick which is closest to your own system):

   (a) ward sister received verbal reports from all nurses on the morning shift on the work they have been responsible for carrying out
   (b) ward sister receives verbal work reports from team leaders on the morning shift on the work their teams have carried out
   (c) nurses write up nursing Kardex or sign work lists when work is completed and only report on any important changes in patients to ward sister
   (d) there is no organized system of reporting back on work in the ward

SECTION 3: SURVEY LIST

Knowledge

1. Do you feel that your general/psychiatric nursing training has prepared you adequately for the care of elderly patients?

   Yes No Don't know

2. Do qualified nurses working on your ward require special post-basic training to care for the elderly?

   Yes No Don't know

3. Do you feel there are any areas in wards' nursing where more education and training should be carried out?

Yes No Don't know

If yes, which areas?

Skill utilization

1. Did you choose to come and work with the elderly on this ward? (please tick one response)
   (a) had no real choice, it was where they had a trained staff vacancy
   (b) had no choice at all
   (c) not really, it just happened that way
   (d) yes definitely, have always wanted to work with elderly people
   (e) yes, it was the most convenient job at the time
   (f) other reasons

2. In your present situation do you feel that good use is being made of your skills? (please tick)

SKILL	UTILIZATION				
	Very little use	*Little use*	*Some use*	*Good use*	*Very good use*
Basic nursing skills	....	....	......	......	....
Rehabilitation skills	....	....	......	......	....
Technical nursing skills	....	....	......	......	....
Management skills	....	....	......	......	....
Teaching skills	....	....	......	......	....
Communication skills	....	....	......	......	....

3. Is there anything about your job that makes you really satisfied or gives you a feeling of accomplishment or achievement?

Yes No

If yes, please tell me what it is.

Rehabilitation concept

1. How would you define the term 'rehabilitation'? (What does it involve?)

2. Please tell me what you consider to be the essential parts of an active rehabilitation programme of nursing care for:

   (a) those patients on your ward who are termed 'rehabilitation patients'
   (b) those patients who are termed 'long-stay/continuing care patients'

3. What is the nurse's role in the rehabilitative care of her/his patients?

APPENDIX B: NOTES OF THE FIRST QUALITY CIRCLE MEETING

Date .... Name of note taker ....

Time ....

Location ....

1. Those present (Facilitator)
   (indicate person selected as leader)

2. Those who have apologized for absence

3. Outline of Quality Circle and questions raised
   - Outline of Quality circle available from Bill Lemmer
   - Tick the box if all members of Circle have copies of programme and guidelines

   ☐

4. Agreed time limit ....

5. All issues/problems raised
   (Mark with p = practical/realistic, or ip = impractical/unrealistic when decision is made)

6. Issue/problem to be tackled

7. Work for next meeting

8. Date and time of next meeting

(Signed) ....

(Leader) (Facilitator) (Note taker)

Tuckman, B.W. (1965) Developmental sequence in small groups. *Psychol. Bull.*, **63**, 384–99.

Yalom, I.D. (1975) *The Theory and Practice of Group Psychotherapy*, 2nd edn, Basic Books, New York.

APPENDIX A: THERAPEUTIC NURSING FUNCTION INDICATOR

Sisters' questionnaire (Tooting Bec Hospital)

INTRODUCTION

This questionnaire will be administered at the beginning and end of the Sisters' Group. It is intended to provide an evaluation of how beneficial this Sisters' Group has been.

Please complete the questionnaire and return it at the next Sisters' Group meeting. The questionnaire is totally confidential and will not be directly attributed to individuals.

Please follow the instructions for each question. Where a question asks you to tick, tick the appropriate number(s) or letter(s):

1 √ g √

SECTION 1: GOAL CONTENT

1. How would you describe nursing in your ward? (What does your nursing involve?)

2. Which of the following activities takes up most time on your ward? Please rank the activities listed below from 1–8 (1 being that activity which takes up most time and 8 that which takes up least of your time):

   (a) feeding patients, assisting patients with food
   (b) washing patients (not bathing)
   (c) caring for incontinent patients – washing, changing, cleaning
   (d) toileting, commoding, toilet training
   (e) dressing, undressing patients
   (f) caring for pressure areas
   (g) exercising immobile patients
   (h) communicating with patients

3. Many nurses working with the elderly have described their work as involving the following activities. Again, please rank activities in order of importance from 1 to 8:

   (a) carrying out medical treatment prescribed by the doctor
   (b) getting patients to move around and become more mobile
   (c) trying to teach and encourage patients to do things for themselves
   (d) keeping patients clean and comfortable
   (e) trying to create a relaxed atmosphere on the ward where patients feel 'at home'
   (f) caring for the physical needs of patients
   (g) stimulate patients to take an interest in surroundings and themselves
   (h) observing and recording medical progress of patients

SECTION 2: PRESCRIPTION/ORGANIZATION AND PLANNING OF NURSING CARE

Method of organizing work on the ward

1. What type of information do you make sure is collected from your patients to help assess and plan their nursing care?

2. How do you collect this information?

3. Who is responsible for collecting this information from the patients?

4. Now that this information is collected, where is it stored on the ward?

5. How do nurses working on the ward get access to this information?

6. What do you do with this information when it is collected?

7. Do you use structured Nursing Care Plans to organize care for each patient on your ward?

8. When you have identified the nursing problems of your patients do you:
   (a) inform your nursing staff and make a note of the problem(s) in the Kardex?
   (b) list the problems and offer nursing measures to cope with them?
   (c) make a written record of the problem on the Nursing Care Plan and offer nursing actions to solve them?
   (d) carry on with the ward routine (most patient problems can be dealt with in the daily routine of care)?
   (e) carry on with the ward work observing for changes in the patient's condition and noting any change?

9. Do you usually set time limits within which you can expect problems to be solved?

   always – noted in the Nursing Care Plan
   usually – written or expressed verbally
   sometimes – keep a mental note of the situation
   rarely – just don't know how things develop
   never

10. How do you monitor the progress of your patients' conditions in relation to their nursing needs?

11. How do staff on the ward obtain information regarding the day-to-day progress and care of their patients? (please tick)

    (a) daily nursing round with Sister
    (b) direct involvement in the planning and organizing of patient care by all grades of staff
    (c) reference to the nursing Kardex (individually reading and writing up of reports and care given)
    (d) reference to the nursing Kardex (collectively at report sessions in morning/afternoon/evening)
    (e) information communication of information between staff during work
    (f) reference to patient progress chart attached to nursing care plans
    (g) reference to information worksheets

Active management cycle

1. How do you inspect the daily needs of your patients? (please tick)

   (a) gather up information from various sources about each patient as best you can
   (b) make a point of seeing those patients who are ill and whose condition needs more careful consideration before delegating care
   (c) check on/monitor patients' conditions while performing other jobs, e.g. medicine rounds, rounds with the nursing officer or medical rounds
   (d) check on/monitor patients' progress while performing routine ward work with other members of staff
   (e) make a point of going round each patient every morning/coming on duty and discussing their condition with them
   (f) rely mainly on written reports and information from nursing staff during duty hours to monitor patients' needs.

2. Which of the following methods of prescribing nursing work is closest to the system used on this ward?

   (a) there is a system of ward task lists in the form of procedure books, ward lists, and duties for nurses
   (b) there is a set routine of work which everyone knows about
   (c) there is a Kardex sheet for each patient where instructions and comments are written in by ward sister and nurses caring for patients
   (d) there are individual worksheets for each patient, updated by ward sister each day which set out details of care for the patient

2. Please tell me what you consider to be the essential parts of an active rehabilitation programme of nursing care for:

   (a) those patients on your ward who are termed 'rehabilitation patients'
   (b) those patients who are termed 'long-stay/continuing care patients'

3. What is the nurse's role in the rehabilitative care of her/his patients?

APPENDIX B: NOTES OF THE FIRST QUALITY CIRCLE MEETING

Date .... Name of note taker ....

Time ....

Location ....

1. Those present (Facilitator)
   (indicate person selected as leader)

2. Those who have apologized for absence

3. Outline of Quality Circle and questions raised
   - Outline of Quality circle available from Bill Lemmer
   - Tick the box if all members of Circle have copies of programme and guidelines

   ☐

4. Agreed time limit ....

5. All issues/problems raised
   (Mark with p = practical/realistic, or ip = impractical/unrealistic when decision is made)

6. Issue/problem to be tackled

7. Work for next meeting

8. Date and time of next meeting

(Signed) ....

(Leader) (Facilitator) (Note taker)

NOTES OF THE SECOND QUALITY CIRCLE MEETING

Date .... Name of note taker ....

Time ....

Location ....

1. Those present (Facilitator)
   (Leader)
   (Note taker)

2. Those who have apologized for absence

3. Options for resolving issue (record all)

4. Action to be taken

5. Aims/goals of action

6. Each member's contribution

7. Evaluation ideas

8. Action plan and goals written down separately: Yes No

9. Date and time of next meeting

(Signed) ....

(Facilitator) (Leader) (Note taker)

NOTES OF THE THIRD QUALITY CIRCLE MEETING

Date .... Name of note taker ....

Time ....

Location ....

1. Those present (Facilitator)
   (Leader)
   (Note taker)

2. Those who have apologized for absence

3. Results of action taken by individual members

4. Evaluation of action taken

5. Has the issue been resolved?

6.

Date and time of next meeting

(Signed) ....

(Facilitator) (Leader) (Note taker)

NOTES OF THE FOURTH QUALITY CIRCLE MEETING

Date .... Name of note taker ....

Time ....

Location ....

1. Those present

2. Those who have apologized for absence

3.

Date and time of next meeting

(Signed) ....

(Facilitator) (Leader) (Note taker)

— 5 —
Making decisions about research

5.1 INTRODUCTION

Health care providers are no different from other providers of services to people when it comes to the necessity of questioning what they are doing.

In the past few years the attention of many in the health service has been sharply focused by the questions raised in the Griffiths Report (1984):

> We are seeking to ensure that the expenditure devoted to the Health Service does reach its target: Improvement in the physical and mental health of the people and in the prevention, diagnosis and treatment of illness.

The nursing profession is not new to the idea of questioning. Working in a health authority encompassing the Nightingale School, the words of Florence Nightingale (1859) ring in our ears: 'Practical work without science is like the pilot of a ship without compass and a rudder. Practical work must be based on good theory which sums up the difficulties of current practice.' But perhaps it was not until relatively recently that nurses began to appreciate not only the need to question all aspects of their work, but also the necessity of providing objective answers.

In mental health care nurses are now faced with questions such as: how many nurses do you need? What are the benefits of using nurses to provide a service? Why do we need Community Psychiatric Nurses (CPNs)? Without the evidence to support their answers to these and other questions, nurses frequently lose credibility and, in some cases, their jobs.

In its Code of Professional Conduct, the United Kingdom Central Council for Nursing, Midwifery and Health Visiting (UKCC, 1984) outlines how the nurse, in whatever speciality they work, should exercise professional accountability. Items 2 and 3 state that each nurse shall:

> Ensure that no act or omission on his/her part or within his/her sphere of influence is detrimental to the condition and safety of patients and clients;
> Take every reasonable opportunity to maintain and improve professional knowledge and competence. (p. 2)

It is interesting to reflect how these and other items of the code are interpreted by nurses. In the job descriptions that West Lambeth Health Authority currently gives to its sisters and charge-nurses it states:

'1. Authority and responsibility.
  (f) Develop methods for evaluating and continuously monitoring methods of care;
  (j) Assess current nursing research and its application to the specific area of care.'

If your job description does not say anything about these demands in relation to asking and answering questions, John Wells (1985) at the Institute of Advanced Nurse Education suggests the following addendum should be added to it:

> To search for excellence in nursing care through a research minded approach critically analysing the care given by oneself and others for whom one is responsible and to seek objective research evidence to warrant persuance or change in given care. (p. 3)

This 'search for excellence' is a key component in many post-basic education courses available to nurses. Considerable importance in nursing is attached to the business of asking questions and providing objective answers to these questions. However, it is not sufficient for those directly involved in giving the service to proclaim such importance. We need to know what it means for those involved in the direct provision of care, and knowing this, we then need to facilitate and support them.

The UKCC Code of Conduct, referred to earlier, implies that all nurses, most particularly those whose work brings them into face-to-face contact with patients, need to do two things. First whatever they are doing they need to ask the basic questions:

How?
Why?
What happens if?
Do I know what I am doing?
Is this the best way?
And crucially, what are the effects on the patients?

Second they need to find the answers to these questions. If the answers are unknown or negative, then the Code of Conduct suggests that we should not continue that course of action. If we then do continue, we act at our own and the patients' peril and open ourselves to charges of professional misconduct and negligence. Put in these terms, the practitioner of nursing begins to understanding the importance of questioning and answering.

5.2 PERSPECTIVES

Throughout this book we draw on the experience gained during work on the five psychogeriatric wards. At the beginning of this book it was abundantly clear from participant observation that the nurses on these wards had not begun taking the first step in asking questions about their own practice.

The scenario was all too familiar, and is described in greater detail in Chapter 6. Typically, care was being given in an unthinking way, was governed by a rigid routine and an orientation to tasks of care. Yet frequently, both during observation periods and later during interviews, nurses of all grades demonstrated their ability to ask questions. Most commonly they would question staffing levels, equipment purchase, and other management issues. The problem appeared to be an inability to look at their own practice.

Nurses wherever they work continually encounter the problem of translating theory into practice, whether it be a new practice policy or the weight of research evidence (see e.g. Norton *et al.*, 1975, on pressure sore prevention in the elderly). In the final analysis it is often the constraint of having to provide a service, there and then within the available resources, that determines how much theory goes into practice. Getting up 28 elderly, confused people, washed, dressed, and fed with three staff (just one qualified) before 8 a.m. determines a strict routine and task orientation to care. It might be argued, and indeed is by some of the ward staff, that allocation of task is the most efficient (not effective) method of carrying out care in these circumstances.

Throughout the work we, and the others who supported the project, always came back to asking the question: 'What does it mean to the people working on the wards?' Therefore, it was no surprise that this was the key question when we came to talk about our approach to evaluating the project.

When put alongside discussions in Chapter 4, and in the introduction to this chapter, we have a clear idea of the principles guiding our approach to the work:

1. Groupwork as the focus of the educational intervention;
2. Constant mindfulness of 'where people were at';
3. The importance of asking questions and answering them objectively particularly in relation to practice.

5.3 USING RESEARCH

At the start of any new initiative, it is obvious that those involved need to have a clear idea of where the initiative is going and an understanding of the situation into which change is being introduced. Increasingly, and again given impetus by the changes following Griffiths (1984), those involved in care are being asked to demonstrate how what they are doing is producing results.

Therefore, it was not difficult for us to decide that the work of managing change in the five wards needed to be supported by the kind of objective evidence provided by research. There were, however, difficulties in deciding what methods to use to produce information that we could use and with whom and where to do the research.

In addressing the latter issue, we found it very helpful to use the Donabedian (1969) framework. Although developed as a framework for evaluating the quality of care, we used it to help us decide

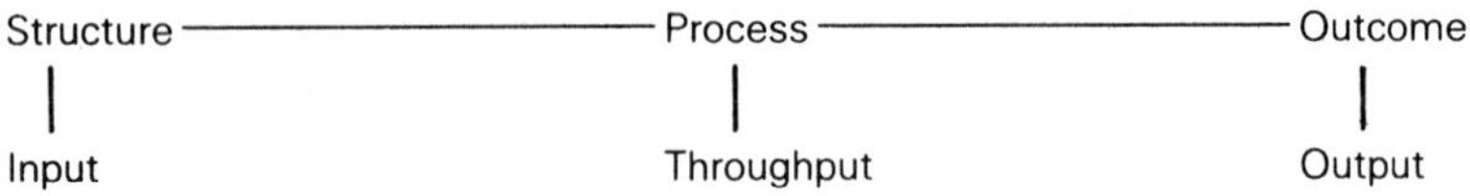

Fig. 5.1 The Donabedian framework.

where to focus our attention. In his work, Donabedian suggests three components be considered (Fig. 5.1).

Each of these components requires its own different approach and research methods.

5.4 OUTCOMES

In our initial steering group meetings we all felt a pressure to concentrate our efforts on outcome evaluation, i.e. on the results of the care given. It is, of course, the component that is central to a medical model of research. Clark (1983), in her book on community health, also identifies the pressure nursing is under to follow this 'classical' method of evaluation. If we in the Management of Change Project could show that what we were doing actually improved care outcomes, the world would indeed be our oyster.

In outcome evaluation what one is doing, in simple terms, is comparing achievements in care against the stated objectives for that care. Although that is nothing new to nursing, for the nursing process itself demonstrates essentially the same idea, there are problems, as follows.

Measuring outcomes

There are examples of attempts to measure outcome in mental health. Beck *et al.* (1984) suggest that the criteria to be measured are the patient's orientation to time, place, and person, and his/her responsibility for activities of daily living once discharged from hospital. But how easy would it be to use these criteria on the psychogeriatric wards of our study, where there might be little change in orientation and few, if any, discharges except through death? There are assessment procedures for the elderly; Pettie and Gilleard

(1979) have produced a manual of the Clifton Assessment Procedures for the Elderly, known as CAPE. But the complexity of using these psychometric tests, and the sensitivity of them in this particular setting, meant that we could not use them.

Appropriateness of data

When we looked at the outcome measures, we questioned how relevant were the criteria to our sample of patients on these long-stay psychogeriatric wards. Consider, for example, Beck *et al.*'s (1984) responsibility for activities of daily living.

Sensitivity of the measure

We could find no examples of outcome measures used to evaluate an educational component in these types of ward. In looking at the changes we expected from our educational input, we constantly questioned whether the measures available would detect changes in the way in which care was given. Eventually, we speculated, changes in perception and attitude among the staff might improve the health status of the people they cared for, but how long would this take? Before that, we hoped to identify changes in the perceptions, attitudes, and values of the nurses and possibly the quality of care.

Attributing cause to effect

Given a change in outcome or the achievement of objectives over a period of time, there might be many contributing factors, from simple elements such as change in diet to more complex inputs like occupational therapy. Thus, to prove our case using an outcome measure, we would need to control for all other possible factors affecting outcome. As Given *et al.* (1979) point out: 'the relationship between process and outcome variables is frequently obscured by failing to control for intervening variables.' (p. 87)

Notwithstanding these problems, we concluded that a focus on outcome evaluation would be our ideal choice. Given the scarcity of appropriate, ready-to-use instruments the way forward would be to work up our own standards and criteria, and to try to test these and use them as outcome measures. A patient's Bill of Rights was the first fruit of this work (see Chapter 8); however, it became clear that much work needed to be done to refine and test this or any other measure that we might produce.

Discussions about outcome measures kept returning to the conviction that we should use the nurses on the wards as a resource in developing a measure. Even our own Bill of Rights of Standards Document would be to a large extent a 'top-down' approach. The result was that we postponed any attempt to measure outcome until later when more work would be done with the people involved in care on the wards.

5.5 STRUCTURE

By a structural component, Donabedian (1969) intended all factors associated with the setting in which care is taking place: the physical facilities, equipment, staffing levels, and organizational structure. In mental health the Welsh Office (1978) have produced a Model Standards Document for hospitals for the mentally ill and the mentally handicapped. Known as the Nodder Report, this document provides a set of structural standards and a checklist for such institutions. As a measure of standards for the environment in which care takes place, it is particularly useful. However, it says nothing about the effectiveness of the care actually given in that environment.

Thus a structural approach unrelated to other components has little, if any, value to patient care. Clark (1983) argues that the weakness of this approach in isolation is the assumption that if the structure is good, good care will follow and vice versa. This is just not the case.

On the wards involved in our work a Nodder checklist had been used to assess the environment in the past. We, therefore, did not consider further adapting a structural approach.

5.6 PROCESS

The discussions we had were more extensive and less clear-cut than has been outlined here, but at the end of the day we all had a strong feeling for a focus on the process of care. It was recognized that at some stage any project concerned with the management of change would have to include an evaluation of all three components and examine their interrelationship.

In looking at the process of care giving, we were interested in how the educational activities influenced the approach to care. Our question was becoming clearer. What effect, if any, does our educational input have on the attitudes and perceptions of those at whom it is directed? Increasingly this is the question that all nurse teachers are having to answer.

Having focused on the question, we then considered how we might answer it. We found several ready-to-use process measures. Few had been used in mental health and most were American in origin. Outside mental health Qualpacs (Wandelt and Ager, 1974), Monitor (Godstone *et al.*, 1983), and Nursing Audit (Phaneuf, 1972) appeared to be the most popular process tools. In reviewing them, we came across several anticipated problems of using them in our setting:

1. They represented a 'top-down' approach;
2. The criteria were inappropriate to the setting;
3. They were not sensitive enough to detect small changes;
4. They were not tried and tested in this setting.

Therefore, we opted for a different sort of approach to process evaluation.

5.7 CHOOSING AN APPROACH TO EVALUATION

In the space of a few pages in this book, then, many important decisions have been made about using research. The process here required much brainstorming, thought, and discussion. The further the debate went on, the higher and more demanding became our expectations of the research. It was clear that no one method of collecting information would provide all that was required. In retrospect, it seemed a fairly straightforward decision to choose a multiplicity of methods. But in practice, it was a lengthy and difficult process.

For many nurses research is seen as an academic exercise done in high places by bright people. Nursing has been described as a mixture of myth, mystery, and magic, and to most nurses research is all three.

The discussions threw up concerns that the information would not be accessible until the project was completed. In Chapters 8 and 9 we explore in depth the collaborative nature of the work on the five wards. In our work it was obvious that just as education and management were expected to contribute in a very real way to care on the wards, so was research. Any research we did had to be accessible to all those involved and removed from the domain of myth, mystery, and magic.

5.8 ACTION RESEARCH

In a fairly naïve way we have been arguing the relevance of what Lathleen and Farnish (1984) call a 'classical' (natural science) model of research vs a more 'anthropological' (social science) model. They further identify that this is a reflection of the wider debate about the nature of the social sciences. Our discussions firmly put us with those who Shipman (1981) describes as belonging to the 'bottom-up' social sciences, concentrating on the way humans construct models of the social world.

There is increasing support for the adoption of this sort of perspective in nursing. 'Action research' is a term that has been used to describe one such approach. Greenwoood (1984) views it as the most appropriate method for nursing research. Towell (1979) neatly sums up how action research works: 'work carried out in a collaborative relationship with practitioners in which the intention is both to contribute to the resolution of practical problems and to increase understanding of the issues being studied' (p. 117). There have been many different attempts to describe what action research is (Lewin, 1948; Cherns, 1969). In adopting this approach, we perhaps share Elliott and Ebbutt's (1983) view of it as 'a mode of reflection which enables professional development'.

In adopting this framework, we have seen it as operating much as Kurt Lewin (1948) describes as a 'spiral of circles':

1. Identifying the issue/question;
2. Collecting information/fact finding;
3. Joint action planning;
4. Implementing the action planned;
5. Revision of the question/issue.

As we report in Chapter 6, we used this cycle four times in the work on the five wards. This approach has enabled us to:

1. See issues from the practitioners' perspective; we were able to understand how the individual nurses on the wards understood and perceived their situation;
2. Collaborate closely as educator, researcher, practitioner, and manager;
3. Continually evaluate how the project was progressing, and to utilize this information in developing new strategies;
4. Continually feedback information to the people concerned; enabling them to take more responsibility for the issue or problem and use that constructively in their own situation.

5.9 DIFFERENT METHODS

We have already defined the need for a multiplicity of methods in collecting the information required. During each of the cycles mentioned different ways of evaluating care were tried. At the end of each phase (cycle) of the project the information collected was analysed and used in reformulating the issues and action plan. We also took the opportunity to examine the research method employed, its strengths and weaknesses, and to make decisions about how to proceed in the next phase.

Although different methods were examined in depth, the wealth of texts on the research process (e.g. Cormack, 1984; Treece and Treece, 1977) and research methods (e.g. Moser and Kalton, 1971) it is useful to look at the methods we utilized in our study and make some general comments about them.

Observation

The origins of the project are described earlier, but here it is important to note that when Bill Lemmer came into the organization, it was from a very different environment, namely that of the Cassel Hospital. Therefore, it was necessary to take stock of that new environment.

One of the best ways of doing this was to go on to the wards and there to work with the ward teams. It was an ideal opportunity to collect information. As Fox (1976) states, 'the best way to learn about a complex interpersonal situation is to watch it', (p. 198). The process of nursing on wards is certainly a complex matter. In other ways it was also beneficial to the project: it helped to establish the relationship between teacher/researcher and practitioner; and it gave the teacher credibility and provided a real 'feel' for the situation.

Of course, there are difficulties. One of the key problems is the ethics of the situation, as highlighted by Treece and Treece (1977) in their chapter on observation. It is an issue we encountered time and again in the project, and one we shall return to later on. In the case of participant observation, we were careful to ask permission of each ward sister and, through them, the ward teams. The explanation given was simple and honest, describing the work of the training officer and his need to see for himself what it was really like working in the wards.

Fox (1977) talks about the problem that 'watching a research situation often changes it'. Part of the difficulty here is eliminated by the researcher being accepted as part of the team, and although in our case the team were aware of the researcher being engaged in 'finding out', they did not appear to view this negatively. It is interesting to note that nurses generally seem to treat observers with suspicion. Inevitably the researcher does have an influence on the situation; an essential component of participant observation is contributing to care and a qualified nurse with a postgraduate diploma has much to contribute. Thus, it is the basis of the work in managing change and part of our approach.

Another of the difficulties, and indeed one of the major criticisms levelled at observational research, is that it is seen to lack objectivity, reliability, and validity, as Hockey (1985) has mentioned in her humorous book. One of the ways in which we were able to overcome these difficulties was by checking out what we were observing with the people involved in the situation. Second, we were able to use other methods and to compare findings, an observation that the care was task-oriented being confirmed by those providing the care.

We would also question whether objectivity, validity, and reliability really are basic issues in action research. After all, we were deliberately trying to describe the situation from the perspectives of those involved. Pedler (1974) describes action research as 'a process which does not pretend to be objective and which involves the objects of the research in the process itself' (p. 5). Lathleen and Farnish (1984) quote Walker (1980) as saying that there are two kinds of educational researcher: 'He may enter the system to seek truth through explanation, or alternatively, he may enter to seek truth through the portrayal of reality' (p. 31).

What we have attempted throughout the work is a portrayal of the reality for those involved. Although here we return to the ongoing debate between natural sciences and the social sciences, it is worth commenting on the generalizability of the work. The work is specific, individual, and unique, but if readers believe it to ring true, or that bits of it are recognizable in their own situation, then one is able to generalize the findings from the relevant parts of our work. We will argue later in Chapter 9 that the way in which we have approached the work is a model for facilitating change elsewhere. It was not, however, the theoretical arguments that caused the greatest problems, but rather the very practical problem of participant observation taking time. Within the context of a job that required commitments to teaching, this finally meant abandoning participant observation in favour of shorter periods of non-participant observation, where observations could be made in a short space of time without having to give time to participating in care. The participant observation had in fact fulfilled its purpose: the researcher had established credibility and collected a large amount of data for future reference.

While Hockey (1985) talks about the human limitations in observation of any kind and the 'eternal' problems of clear definitions, our observation was unstructured and free from any format. This allowed the researcher to record exactly what happened rather than to try first to categorize it. There is still the danger that certain actions might be interpreted wrongly by the observer, but checking out observations with the observed helps to reduce this source of bias.

Interviewing

Having taken a closer look at how the nursing operated on the wards, it seemed that it would now be a good time to obtain the views of individual nurses of all grades. At this stage of the project, we had a lot of information about the ways in which nursing was done on the wards and more limited information on how nurses viewed it. We were still concerned about imposing our ideas on the situation, and therefore we deliberately opted for a semi-structured interview schedule. There were a dozen or so general questions and an open discussion.

One of the lessons learned from this exercise was how demanding, in terms of time and energy expended, interviewing is (Treece and Treece, 1977). Another of the interesting points to come out of this work was that nurses of all grades have a great deal to say about their work attitudes and perceptions.

There seemed to be numerous advantages in conducting the interviews, perhaps the principal ones being that: they gave the nurses working on the wards a sense of being valued and that their opinions counted; and they developed and consolidated the relationship of teacher/researcher and practitioner.

Questionnaires

Following the observation and interviewing, we had a solid baseline of information about approaches to nursing care on the wards. Two phases of the project had been completed and we now had clearer ideas about the educational input. A course of action had been planned (see Chapters 4 and 6) in groupwork on each of the five wards facilitated by teachers.

There were several questions that we wanted to ask about this course of action. The central question was, again, that of what effects, if any, the educational input had had on the way in which the nurses on the wards approached their work. Here it was suggested that some form of before-and-after evaluation was required, and the problem was which instruments to use to capture any change that might have taken place.

We again reviewed the available instruments. There were problems with the language and the lack of reporting or use in the UK of Qualpacs and Nursing Audit, particularly in psychiatry, where we found no evidence of use; however, the issue that gave us most concern was that of the standards and criteria implicit in each instrument. Analysis of the statements and cues suggest a standard of care different from, and in applicable cases too high for, our setting. We suspected that these and other instruments would not provide a measure of what was really happening on the wards; nor would they be sensitive enough to detect changes that might be occurring.

We decided that in an ideal world we would generate our own standards and criteria and use these as the basis for measurement. Time and resources did not permit us to explore the ideal; thus, we opted for a pre- and post-questionnaire approach. There was much in favour of us using the questionnaire method:

1. We already had a wealth of data to use in constructing the questionnaire;
2. It is a relatively simple, inexpensive, and less time-consuming method of collecting data;
3. The results can be easily analysed using a computer;
4. Respondents can remain anonymous.

As we intended to administer it twice, once at the beginning and end of a six-month period, these were important considerations. The advantages outweighed the major disadvantages that we could identify:

1. Lack of in-depth information;
2. The respondent may choose to omit questions without explanation;
3. The nature of the questions may force people to choose a response that is not representative or deliberately falsify information;
4. Some questions might be misunderstood.

There are many other advantages and disadvantages to questionnaires, but these have been well expanded elsewhere (e.g. Moser and Kalton, 1971; Cormack, 1984).

We encountered problems that people often identify with questionnaires such as non-responses, misunderstanding, and difficulty putting the information on the computer. In Chapter 6 we show how the two questionnaires helped us to demonstrate that change was taking place. In the real world of the present-day health service, it helped to answer criticisms of the nurses and other health care workers and of others who assert that the only valid way to do research is by using quantitative methods.

Diaries

During the same period that the staff were completing questionnaires we were interested to know how the facilitators of the groupwork viewed their sessions. It was decided that the best way to capture this information would be to keep an open format diary in which each facilitator could record their views on each session that they facilitated. The diary was intended to be purely descriptive and provide a subjective insight into the workings of the groups.

The data gathered were rich in quality and provided much material for discussion. As with much of the information we collected, it was open to view to all the nurses working on the wards. And as with virtually all diary studies a problem highlighted by Hockey (1985) – entries were missed following some of the sessions. In addition, on several occasions information was recorded a considerable time after the sessions, and we can only speculate on the amount of information lost.

Quality Circles

For the fourth and final phase of the project, we were looking for a method of collecting information with which the wards could continue, once our particular project was completed. The methods we have talked about so far require a certain amount of research knowledge and expertise to run them, and to get information from them. When the project finished, these resources would no longer be available.

From work elsewhere in the health authority we became aware of Quality Circles and their value; we investigated further and it appeared to us that here was a method to suit our needs. The literature on quality circles is extensive both inside the health service (Hyde, 1984; Johnson and Clarke, 1984; Davis, 1986; Lorentzon and Osborne, 1985) and outside (Robson, 1984; Hutchins, 1980; Lorenz, 1981). We found the following points to be of importance:

1. They allowed for the development of the individual;
2. They facilitated the development of a team;

3. They develop the concept of consensus;
4. They solve problems;
5. They encourage a research-minded attitude;
6. They help to facilitate change.

We will discuss in greater depth how they helped us to action change in Chapter 6.

Needless to say, we made mistakes that ultimately affected the success of the quality circle programme. Not enough time and resources were put into the preparation of people for the circles. We had particular problems with the roles of leader and facilitator: in some circles this led to individuals taking control and inhibiting other members (Robson, 1984). On the whole, the quality circles produced some exciting innovations and changes demonstrating that they were a useful choice.

Therapeutic Nursing Function Indicator

The work done during the first three phases of the project led us to those conclusions that many other researchers have reached (e.g. Fretwell, 1982), namely that the role of the ward sister is crucial and is of central importance to the delivery of nursing care. The groupwork of the fourth and final phase of the project was therefore partly focused on them. Regular Sisters' Groups are described elsewhere (Chapters 4 and 6). Alongside the groupwork, we wanted to evaluate how far it had facilitated change.

The work of Kitson (1984, 1986) had impressed us greatly, and we thought we could usefully apply her Therapeutic Nursing Function Indicator (TNF) to the sisters on our wards. In a similar way to the questionnaires, we decided to apply it at the beginning and end of a six-month period of educational input into the Sisters' Group.

As its name implies, the TNF was devised to identify those sisters who provide a therapeutic (i.e. patient-centred) intervention, in comparison with those who do not. The instrument itself comprises a list of statements to which the sister responds and is scored on. We speculated that if our educational programme was in any way successful, sisters' scores over the six months would show an increase.

Although Kitson's work was with geriatric-ward sisters, we had little to do in adapting it for use with our sisters in the psychogeriatric wards. The author herself gave us advice and support. In her work, Kitson had gone on to relate her TNF to a Nursing Function Matrix, which attempted to measure the quality of care patients were receiving on the geriatric wards:

> The results showed that quality of care seemed to be related more to the orientation and perception of the ward sister than any other number of extraneous variables such as medical and paramedical input, ward facilities and ancillary staff support. (Kitson, 1986, p. 133)

At last on the final lap of the project, we were beginning to move from pure process evaluation to look at quality on the edge of the Donabedian component of outcome.

5.10 CONCLUSION

The discussions of this chapter have illustrated how we have interwoven research and evaluation into the business of managing change. We have demonstrated its importance and how it forms an essential part of the change process. When we propose a model for change (Chapter 9), research and evaluation will figure prominently; it must also be clear that a great deal of thought and discussion goes into deciding how best to answer the questions posed.

Because of the nature of the work, we have argued the case for a 'bottom-up' approach where the practitioner is a partner in the process. Donabedian's framework (1969) has been utilized to help us decide how to approach the issues, and here it is an important point that we did not start at the outcome end of the continuum. Increasingly there seems to be pressure to start evaluating using outcomes.

In deciding how to approach the research, we have adopted an action research framework, and argued the case for its use in health care research, particularly nursing research. By the end of this book, we think it will be abundantly clear that this decision was a major factor in the success we had.

In response to different situations, we have shown the use of a variety of different research tools, some well known, others not so; details of all these methods can be found in the literature cited. In this chapter we have deliberately attempted to examine the process of deciding how best to proceed with research and how these decisions are reached. The results are described in Chapter 6.

REFERENCES

Beck, C.M. *et al.* (eds) (1984) *Mental Health – Psychiatric Nursing: A Holistic Life-Cycle Approach*, C.V. Mosby, St Louis, MO.

Cherns, A. (1969) Social research and its diffusion, *Human Relations*, **22**(3), 210–18.

Clark, J. (1983) Problems of evaluation in preventive health care, in J. Clark and J. Henderson. *Community Health*, Churchill Livingstone, London, pp. 265–75.

Cormack, D. (1984) *The Research Process in Nursing*, Blackwell Scientific, Oxford.

Davis, C. (1986) *Can Quality Circles Add to the Quality of Care in the Health Service?* King's Fund Paper, March, King Edward's Hospital Fund for London, London.

Donabedian, A. (1969) Some issues in evaluating the quality of care. *American Journal of Public Health*, **59**, 1833–6.

Elliott, J. and Ebbutt, D. (1983) *Action Research into Teaching for Understanding: A Guide to the TIQL Project*, Schools Council, London.

Fox, D.J. (1977) *Fundamentals of Nursing Research*, Appleton- Century-Crofts, New York.

Fretwell, J.E. (1982) *Ward Teaching and Learning*, RCN, London.

Given, B. *et al.* (1979) Relationships of processes of care to patient outcome. *Nursing Research*, **28**(2), March–April, 85–93.

Godstone, L. *et al.* (1983) *Monitor. An Index of the Quality of Nursing Care for Acute Medical and Surgical Wards*, Newcastle Polytechnic Products, Newcastle upon Tyne.

Greenwood, J. (1984) Nursing research; a position paper, *Journal of Advanced Nursing*, **9**, 77–82.

Griffiths, R. (Chairman) (1984) *NHS Management Inquiry*, HMSO, London.

Hockey, E. (1985) *Nursing Research. Mistakes and Misconceptions*, Churchill Livingstone, London.

Hutchins, D.C. (1980) QC Circles: an introduction. *Industrial and Commercial training*, **12**(1), 8–15.

Hyde, P. (1984) Something for everyone. *Nursing Times*, 28 November.

Johnson, D. and Clarke, J. (1984) Developing quality of care. *Nursing Times*, December 5th, pp. 36–7.

Kitson, A. (1984) Steps towards the identification and development of nursing's therapeutic function in the care of the hospitalized elderly.

Unpublished D.Phil. thesis, University of Ulster, Colraine.

Kitson, A. L. (1986) Indicators of quality in nursing care – an alternative approach. *Journal of Advanced Nursing*, **11**, 133–44.

Lathleen, J. and Farnish, S. (1984) *The Ward Sister Training Project*. Nursing Education Research Unit Report No. 3, King's College, University of London.

Lewin, K. (1948) *Resolving Social Conflicts*, Harper and Row, New York.

Lorentzon, M. and Osborne, S. (1985) Quality Circles. *Senior Nurse*, December, pp. 24–6.

Lorenz, C. (1981) The shopfloor's verdict on quality circles. *The Financial Times*, February 2nd, p. 8.

Moser, C. and Kalton, G. (1971) *Survey Methods in Social Investigation*, Heinemann Educational, London.

Nightingale, F. (1859) *Notes on Nursing*, Dinkworth 1950, London.

Norton, D. *et al.* (1975) *Investigation of Geriatric Nursing Problems in Hospital*, Churchill Livingstone, London.

Pedler, M. (1974) An action research approach to training interventions. *Management Education and Development,* **15**, pt 2.

Pettie, A.H. and Gilleard, C.J. (1979) *Manual of the Assessment Procedures for the Elderly (CAPE)*, Hodder and Stoughton, Sevenoaks.

Phaneuf, M.C. (1972) *The Nursing Audit. Profile for Excellence*, Meredith, New York.

Robson, M. (1984) *Quality Circles in Action*, Gower, London.

Shipman, M. (1981) *The Limitations of Social Research*, Longman, London.

Towell, D. (1979) A social systems approach to research and change in nursing care. *International Journal of Nursing Studies*, **16**, 111–21.

Treece, E.W. and Treece, J.W. (1977) *Elements of Research in Nursing*, Mosby, Missouri.

United Kingdom Central Council for Nursing, Midwifery and Health Visiting (UKCC) (1984) *Code of Professional Conduct for Nurses, Midwives and Health Visitors*, UKCC, London.

Walker, R. (1980) The conduct of educational case studies: ethics, theory and procedures, in W.B. Dockerell and D. Hamilton (eds) *Rethinking Educational Research*, Hodder and Stoughton, London, pp. 30–63.

Wandelt, M.A. and Ager, J. (1974) *Quality Patients' Care Scale*, Appleton-Century-Crofts, New York.

Wells, J. (1985) Seminar to Sisters' Professional Development Course, Unpublished paper, Nightingale School, London.

Welsh Office (1978) *Model Standards Document: Hospitals for the Mentally Ill and Mentally Handicapped*, HMSO, London; also *Organisational and Management Problems of Mental Illness Hospitals*, Report of Working Group, HMSO, London, 1980.

— 6 —
Working with change: A case study

6.1 INTRODUCTION

At the end of the book, in Chapter 9, we draw all our discussions together and propose a model for change. Although the model has been 'fine-tuned' and is now in use again in the same setting (see reference to the Model Ward and Training Project in Chapter 8), this chapter provides a feedback from what was the piloting of the model.

It is important to point out that the model we propose is one that can be taken and applied in a variety of contexts. Because in this chapter we present a particular 'case study', it is however a unique example of the model in practice; we have included it here in order to explain how we arrived at our model. It illustrates how facilitating change can work and the difficulties it produces.

6.2 GENERALIZABILITY

The method of approaching the project, action research, described earlier in Chapter 5, does not attempt to seek universal truths and support them with 'scientific' proof, rather it seeks to do the latter of Walker's (1980) suggestions: 'the news the educational researcher brings is generally one of two kinds. He may enter the system in order to seek truth through explanation or alternatively he may enter it to seek truth through the portrayal of reality' (p. 31).

In this chapter we have attempted to present some of the reality of the work we were involved in. Hopefully, some of it will ring true with readers' own experience or circumstances. As Greenwood suggests:

> individual, specific and unique situations can only be recognised as individual, specific, unique situations because they are of a kind; we might reasonably expect, therefore, that some of the findings will be generalisable to other situations of like kind. (Greenwood, 1984, p. 77)

6.3 QUESTIONS

Throughout the work on the five psychogeriatric wards we were interested in answering many different questions. Central to them all was the question (often seen as a challenge) of how much effect, if any, were we having with our educational interventions on the people on these wards (staff and patients). In Chapter 5 we have presented the ways in which we arrived at decisions on answering this central question during each stage of the project. It was a question shared by all involved; frequently we would be asked by a member of the ward teams: 'Bill. . .how are we doing?' Similarly, nurse, managers and educationists would probe and ask us if 'it' was working, were things changing, and by how much? They wanted the evidence to support our answers, and in this chapter we present some of them.

As each stage of the project grew and developed, different questions were asked. Our point of reference was always to go back to the aims of the work, namely:

1. To evaluate attitudes towards patient care and the role perceptions among nursing assistants and qualified nurses;
2. To measure the change that had taken place as a result of management and education input to the wards over six-month periods;
3. To use the data gathered as a baseline for initiating change;
4. To develop professional standards;
5. To design an approach to psychiatric care that could be replicated elsewhere.

6.4 APPROACHES

We have already described how we came to adopt an action research framework for this project (Chapter 5). Adopting this framework meant that the work had two important components, as follows.

Collaboration. Action research demands a collaborative approach. In Chapter 7 we describe the collaborators' input into the project steering group (Fig. 6.1).

Cyclical nature. The Management of Change Project started in 1983 with the appointment of a nursing officer (Bill Lemmer), later to become a tutor, with responsibility for the training of nursing assistants. By the conclusion of the project in August 1986, many phases had been completed. The cyclical nature of action research

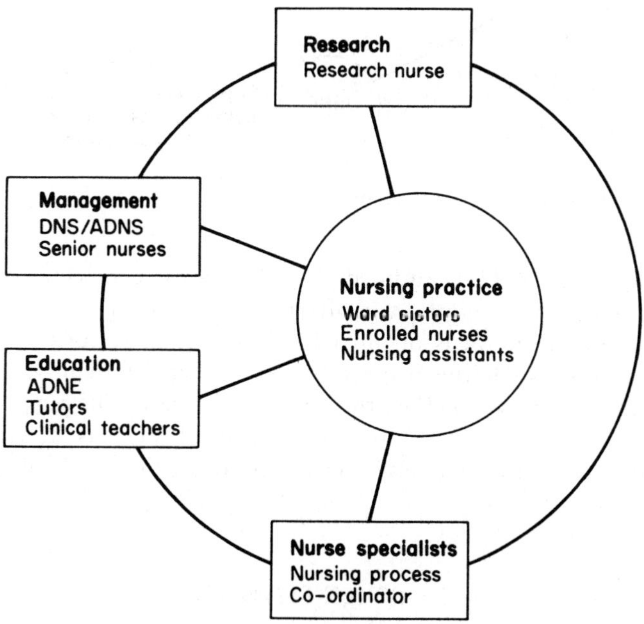

Fig. 6.1 Collaborative nature of project.

described in Chapter 5 (p. 98) meant that many different approaches to educational intervention and evaluation had been tried. In Fig. 6.2 we illustrate how the project developed into distinct phases (equivalent to Lewin's spiral of cycles) and its chronology.

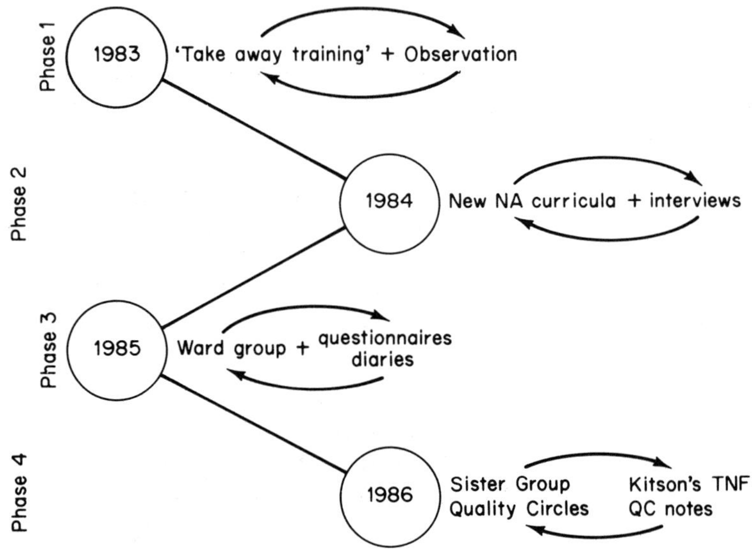

Fig. 6.2 Cyclical nature of the project.

In Chapter 2 we have outlined the educational perspectives that have influenced the work, and progressed in Chapter 3 to discuss groupwork as the focus of our educational interventions.

At each stage of the project we examined different ways of working in groups and chose the most appropriate. The purpose of each of the groups was much as Walton (1971) has described: obtaining relief from anxiety and facilitating attitude and personality change.

6.5 STARTING UP

When you are first appointed to a new job there are a thousand and one questions to ask about the situation you come to and the people you are involved with. Informal discussions, job descriptions, and formal interviews in fact reveal little of the complexities of any new job.

The scenario for the project was set when Bill Lemmer was appointed to his post as in-service training officer for the nursing assistant training programme:

Situation	A large Victorian psychiatric hospital on the outskirts of central London
People	900 in-patients of whom 70% were over 65 years old, with a nursing workforce drawn from the local community and reflecting its multi-ethnic mix; approx. 50% of the workforce was untrained
Current training (unqualified staff)	School-based blocks of one- or two-weeks training.

6.6 THE QUESTIONS

In presenting this work to groups of nurses and other health care workers, one of the techniques we use is 'brainstorming'. Here it is interesting to report some of the questions people would have wanted to ask if they were in Bill's position:

1. *About the nursing assistants*
   How many?
   What were their backgrounds – education?
   – experience?
   – age?
   Do they have job descriptions?
   What do the job descriptions say? Hours of work?
   Where do they work?
   Is there a difference between day and night?
2. *About the in-service training programme*
   What were they taught?
   How are they taught?
   Were the ward staff aware of what they were taught?
   How were they made aware?
   Was what they were taught being practised on the wards?
   How is it evaluated?

Why is there little, if any, evidence that in-service training took place?

3. *About their practice*
   Who are the patients?
   How are they supervised?
   How much supervision?
   Was there any evaluation of their work?
   Did they practise what they were taught?
   What support was available on the ward?
   What is their view about their role?
   How did others see their role?
   What level of work do they do?

Consequently, it is not hard to understand how a project developed. Attempts to answer just a handful of these questions provided the basis for a continuing study. As soon as one finds the answers to the questions that are tackled, one is faced with the dilemma of what to do next: how should one use what has been discovered? Therefore, it seemed appropriate for us to opt for an action research framework (see Chapter 5).

This framework insisted that, first, we collaborate with not just the nursing assistants who were the focus of the work, but also those nursing staff who worked with them and the nurse managers in charge of the wards and units. Second, we had a responsibility to share the answers to the questions we had sought to answer. Third, we had to evaluate and test the action we were taking. Lastly, we had to share the values and beliefs we held about the work.

6.7 BECOMING INVOLVED

The initial stab at answering some of the questions raised was by participant and non-participant observation. In Chapter 5 we have outlined why we chose these methods and their advantages and disadvantages. In this section we illustrate the information and answers they provided.

Bill worked on the wards alongside the nursing assistants for a period of six months. Although this seems a lengthy time there were other ongoing activities. An extensive literature search was undertaken during this period. A partnership with a senior nurse manager developed and a whole range of discussions with people involved took place. On top of this were the teaching commitments of the post both in relation to the nursing assistants and the basic RMN course.

During this period of observation a daily research diary was maintained. The diary makes for some very interesting reading although its observations are those to be made in many of these large psychiatric institutions. To illustrate part of the recorded observations, we want to take two aspects of the nurses' work (early 1983–84).

Routine

A typical day on one of these wards would follow the pattern outlined in Table 6.1. The routine was sacrosanct. If the ward became heavier with highly dependent patients or the staffing levels dropped, for whatever reason, activities would start earlier, so that they could be completed on time. With three staff on duty on the ward of 24 elderly, confused, incontinent patients, the work was often extremely physically demanding and mentally straining. Getting the task done was an efficient way of coping. There was little room for a personal approach to patients by staff. If there were only a sister and two nursing assistants on duty, as was often the case, then everyone 'mucked in'. There was little time for supervision or training.

For the patients, this meant:

1. Being woken early (before waking naturally);
2. Being fed a cup of tea although capable of doing it themselves;
3. Watching others being washed and toileted.

Things could, and did, happen frequently and consistently over which there was little or no individual control. For example,

1. Patients might go without underwear or wear someone else's albeit clean;
2. Their chairs may be tilted back to stop them falling out;
3. They might have to sit in the corner because unruly;
4. They might have a piece of linen tied across their chairs to prevent them getting up;

Table 6.1 The daily routine at the beginning of project (1983)

Time	*Activity*	*Observation*
5.30 a.m. onwards	Patients woken – cup of tea; commoded or sent to toilet; wheeled or walked to be washed or washed by bed; some patients dressed	No privacy; often forced; no choice; not personalised, hospital uniform
7 a.m.	Staff handover; rest of patients got up; rest dressed; patients sat in dayroom, TV/radio on; 'sicker' patients left in bed in dormitory	5 min Very loud; non-selective; very isolated
8 a.m.	Breakfast at tables in living area; medication given; patients sat in living area	Teeth given out at breakfast
10 a.m.	Investigations	
12 midday	Lunch at tables; medication given; patients sat in dayroom; TV/radio on	
1.30 p.m. – 2.30 p.m.	Staff handover	20 min
4 p.m. onwards	Patients got ready for bed	
6 p.m.	Supper at tables; medication given; most patients to bed	Most patients in nightclothes
9 p.m.	Staff handover	

5. The nurse may suddenly leave one patient and not return because of staff shortages elsewhere;
6. They might get no choice in food and sometimes be unable to obtain the food they required;
7. They might wear ill-fitting clothes;
8. They might have to sit on a mobile commode for longer than necessary or longer than was comfortable;
9. They might have an extraordinary number of baths.

At other times things happened so fast that they became disorientated. Acts of urgency, a nurse pushing fast on a wheelchair, were often viewed as threatening by patients, who would verbally and physically attack the staff.

If their eyes were good enough, they would watch a whole range of TV programmes from breakfast TV through Open University items to school programmes, lunchtime news, 'soaps', and children's TV. If they could not see well, the volume was often turned up, so that, like it or not, they could hear. And yet, as we shall see later, the people working on these wards were, on the whole, kind, caring people. The routine, and completion of the routine, was the governing factor. In many ways, the staff of these wards were unthinking and naïve, numbed by the sheer weight of the work, both physically and mentally.

Categorization

The nature of the routine meant that patients not conforming to the task in hand (e.g. patients who tensed their muscles; those who wouldn't walk; or those who could not stay seated) were defined as problems. Patients became named in a non-personal way (e.g. 'that one', 'he's incontinent', 'she's aggressive', 'watch him, he spits', 'hey you, sit down', and 'who's a pretty girl, then?').

Categorization was further emphasized by viewing patients as disease carriers (the terms often being borrowed from the medical diagnosis) (e.g. 'she's demented', 'senile dementia', and 'schizophrenic'). Frequently, at handover, these terms would be used to describe people. In deciding how to care for an individual, these categorizations would be used as an excuse. Thus an incontinent patient would be managed as an incontinent patient rather than trying to assess the causes of the incontinence and promote continence.

So from these two elements of the data we may begin to get a flavour of the care that nursing assistants were involved in. How did it relate to their training? Generally speaking, the nursing assistants could not employ the skills they had acquired, or else the skills were not acquired. First, the nursing assistants did not employ the skills they had acquired. For example, during their programme they were taught about correct lifting techniques.

Once on the wards, a lack of regard for the correct techniques resulted in many cases of back strain or back problems. Second, they were not taught about certain approaches to care, e.g. individualized care. In many cases, had they been so taught, caring would have been diametrically opposed to the values and approaches of the ward nursing. Similar findings were reported by Martin (1984) in his review of fifteen psychiatric hospital enquiries.

6.8 ACTION I

As a result of the observational work and discussions with the staff, four changes were decided upon and implemented:

1. Training became teaching for the whole team in the ward environment;
2. Ward staff became involved in the teaching;
3. Managers became involved in the teaching in the school;
4. The curriculum was changed to include individualized care, interpersonal skills, and communication.

What the nurses think

Coming to a new environment and a new job, one inevitably brings certain values and expectations. Added to this are the skills and abilities one has already gained. It was clear that, in the context of this work, the wards did not put into practice the values and skills held by the training officer – what, then, did they think?

As a second component of becoming involved, interviews were held with all the nursing assistants and the staff involved on the wards. The reason for extending interviews to the staff on the ward was the need to translate theory (what the nursing assistants were taught) into practice. This could not be done without having the trained staff on the wards.

The limitations of the semi-structured interview schedule are dealt with in Chapter 5. Given the limitations, the descriptive data provided helped colour in the picture which was used for the baseline information about this setting. It also provides answers to some of the initial questions that were asked. Again, the amount of

Table 6.2 Nursing assistant interview schedule

A	Please tell me about your experience.
B	Why is this work important to you?
C	What incident or event in patient care stands out in your mind?
D	Please list the nurse–patient 'activities' which concern you most.
E	Can you say what the most difficult part of your job is?
F	What have you learnt in this work?
G	Do you worry about the patients?
H	Do you think it affects us, working in a mental illness hospital?
I	What satisfaction do you get from this work?
J	I've explained the purpose of these questions. Now would you like to ask me any questions?

data are large, and here we give but a few examples of the responses; these are taken from the interviews with 33 nursing assistants on the six elderly mentally ill wards that constituted the sample (the interview schedule is presented in Table 6.2):

(a) *Caring attitudes*

There was no question about the caring nature of the majority of the nursing staff as the following illustrates:

> 'It's the only work I've ever done; I love looking after old people.'
> 'Without us, they wouldn't survive; and without them, we would not have a job.'
> 'It's a need in me, really, caring for people is rewarding.'
> 'I get a lot from this work. Sometimes you're down, you meet people and discuss work and you feel better.'
> 'I like to see days when you can talk to a previously confused patient.'
> 'It's not a rewarding job, but very satisfying. What is mental illness? – it's laughed at on the street but here you understand.'
> 'If I do work, I feel all right. If someone goes [dies], you miss them. They're like a part of the family.'

(b) *Learning*

Three-quarters of the nursing assistants thought that they had learned personal qualities:

understanding
tolerance
patience
older people's needs and illness
compassion
maturity
caring
understanding

While others talked about tasks and procedural skills:

dressing
pulse
drugs
feeding
sections of the Mental Health Act (1982)

(c) *Worry*
Both this question (Table 6.2) and the question about satisfaction seem to indicate some conflict for the nursing assistants in what they would like to be doing and what they are able to do:

> 'Yes, when they're not taking their meal, and when I talk to them and they don't respond.'
> 'Oh yes, very much. If the weather is cold and there's not enough bedding. If I know they're dirty, I change them although there's not time during turnout.'
> 'Yes, we got to worry about their health and safety, they don't even know they are ill.'
> 'Oh yes, I do. If I think something's wrong and someone else says no, I tend to refuse to say it again.'
> 'Yes, you get very attached and they get very poorly.'
> 'Yes, you have to be cruel to be kind.'
> 'Yes, it's petty things. A young woman of 52 – I relate her condition to my own [future].'

The baseline

From both the becoming involved (observation) and what people thought (interviews), several major findings emerge. We can divide these into conflicts for the individual, the approach to care, and success of training (although these also overlap):

(a) *Approaches to care*
Care on these wards can be summarized as routine task-oriented and lacking in individuality. There was little control over the care and little supervision of junior staff. The routine, by and large, dictated the approach.

(b) *Conflict for the individual*
The nursing assistants were relied on heavily, and they were respected and admired by qualified staff as they reduced the burden of care for themselves. The nursing assistants themselves had a caring attitude and were concerned with personal skills and work. However, this concern was dissipated when translated into practice. The routine servicing of patients (production line sounding and appearing) dominated the approach to care.

(c) *Success of training*
Here two factors clearly stood out: practice bore no relation to theory (most evident in nursing assistant's training); and if changes were to be introduced, then all the staff on these wards needed to be involved.

6.9 ACTION II

Although we present the action taken here as a series of summary points, in practice the process of agreeing action took time and included a series of collaborative meetings and paper presentations. The action agreed was as follows:

1. Stop the school-based training for the nursing assistants;
2. Focus on ward-based groupwork;
3. Give a sense of continuity and permanence to the wards by stopping the practice of 'booking out' nurses;
4. Feedback of results to all people involved.

The principles and theory behind groupwork as an approach to education have been discussed in depth in Chapter 4. From the baseline data the focus of this work was to be on:

individuality – establishing patient allocation
control – supervision
– decision-making
– accountability
– continuity

Monitoring change

A lot of work had so far been completed, all of it providing insights. With hindsight, we might have changed the finer details of our method and, perhaps, collected a little less information (we were in danger of being swamped!). However, we were now in a position to move on.

The ward-based training is described elsewhere in this book. Here we present some of the indications we gained that this educational intervention was producing change, and we had two means of doing this. One method was ongoing and provided week-by-week insights into changes occurring on the ward in the diary kept by the facilitators of the ward groups. The second was the questionnaire (see Appendix A to this chapter), designed to elicit the staff's attitudes and perceptions; this was presented to the staff working on the wards at the start and finish of the groupwork programme. Here we give a sample of things that people said; a further selection of comment is appended (Appendices B and C to this chapter).

(a) *The diaries*

Ward	*Date*	*Comment*
5	11/3/85	'Physical environment dramatically changed. Patients sitting in groups. Calendar, orientation cards up, patients joined team meeting. Dormitory more comfortably adorned with names and personal items.
3	13/3/85	'More nursing care being discussed. Pleasure in being more responsible for patients' personal items (toiletries, helping with menu cards)'
2	19/3/85	'Nurse X reports she has been looking after a patient

		when on duty and reported success with her daily supervision and regular toilet programme.'
2	26/3/85	'There was a feeling of ease and accomplishment in the ward team.'

Even by themselves, and given their limitations, the diaries suggest that things were changing, even though changing slowly and following considerable input in terms of skilled personnel – and, of course, not without difficulties and hiccoughs along the way, as other entries in the diary reveal:

Ward	*Date*	*Comment*
1	12/2/85	'Junior staff didn't give respect to senior staff, and the senior staff treated juniors like children – I think we need to work on communication skills.'
2	12/2/85	'There's nothing you can do for these ones, they're all going downhill.'
5	18/2/85	'Enrolled nurse states that it is not possible to give psychological care under pressure of tasks to be done.'
3	18/2/85	'Patients had wool strip tied across the arms of the chairs they were sitting in to prevent them standing and falling when a nurse is not around.

Further examples can be fouind in the appendices to this chapter.

(b) *The questionnaires*

One glance at the questionnaire in the appendices to this chapter is enough to show that a full presentation of the findings is beyond the scope of this book. To illustrate the changes noted, we have taken themes identified as key issues by the work done in the first two stages of the project, namely:

1. individuality in care
2. continuity of care
3. responsibility for care

The data in the next section detail the responses made to two questions on each of these issues.

Individuality in care

How is the nurses' work allocated on your ward? (question 8)

	1st(%)	*2nd*(%)
By having patients to look after	41	72
By everyone doing everything	27	2
Other	32	26

Do you have a choice in which patients you look after? (question 10)

	1st(%)	*2nd*(%)
Yes	10	26
No	86	74

Continuity of care

Do you get the same set of patients to look after? (question 16)

	1st(%)	*2nd*(%)
All the time	29	44
Some of the time	25	30
Varies the whole time	37	22
Other	9	4

Do you think that the care you give your patients is helping them to return to the community? (question 22)

	1st(%)	*2nd*(%)
Yes	41	30
No	49	48

Responsibility for care

Are there nurses on your ward who work harder or less than you?

		1st(%)	*2nd*(%)		1st(%)	*2nd*(%)
Work harder	Yes	12	2	No	69	72
Work less	Yes	27	20	No	25	35

Does the number of staff provided give adequate care? (question 14)

		1st(%)	*2nd*(%)		*1st*(%)	*2nd*(%)
All the care that you would want	Yes	18	6	No	75	85
All basic nursing care	Yes	24	17	No	59	67

We would suggest that the question responses indicate the following:

Question 8 A move towards patient allocation with a corresponding decrease in an everyone-does-everything attitude and task allocation (other).

Question 10 The beginnings of giving nurses choices in the patients they wish to look after, allowing them to become better informed about the patients they choose.

Question 16 More continuity in the care of a patient by allocating each patient for a period of time to one particular nurse.

Question 22 A more realistic view of the care that is provided in these long-stay wards.

Question 13 The beginnings of teamwork; less nurses willing to see themselves as carrying the burden of the work.

Question 14 A greater realization that the care given does not reach the standards the nurses would want.

We would tentatively suggest that there are the signs from the responses outlined here that changes are taking place. In addition, there are the beginnings of a move towards greater individuality, more continuity, and greater responsibility in care.

6.10 ACTION III

We concluded from the diaries and the questionnaires that the group work was effective in facilitating change. We observed that this process was demanding of resources. The facilitators brought with them considerable skills and expertise and gave a couple of hours each week to each ward. The changes observed were over a six-month period and we could only speculate how long it might be before the people involved would be ready for the fast-approaching changes in mental health, e.g. the closure of the hospital.

At this stage, we were also aware that the completion of the project, which had a fixed duration of three years was drawing near. Thus, in addition to the action taken by the ward teams during this phase of the project, we planned for:

1. A Sisters' Group to meet on a regular basis to work through issues;
2. Regular Ward Groups to continue in the form of Quality Circles.

The Sisters' Group was a result of a need to identify a group of people who might take on the work of facilitating change, once the project team had withdrawn. The research of Fretwell (1982), Lathleen and Farnish (1984), and numerous others, should have alerted us to the central role of the ward sister. However, it was not until we began to work with issues of control of care, responsibility for care, and accountability that it really dawned on us that here was the key to success on their wards, namely the ward sister.

Quality Circles seemed to be the ideal option for continuing the groupwork on the wards as they offered structure, were outside normal ward meetings, and we could team up facilitators and circle leaders. To evaluate the success of these proposed actions, we decided to use Kitson's (1985) Therapeutic Nursing Index at the beginning of the Sisters' Group programme and again after six months. We speculated that the rating on the scale should increase if the group had successfully facilitated change. For the Quality Circles we decided to use the circle notes as a research instrument.

6.11 ACTION IV

The end of the project marked the beginning of several initiatives elsewhere in the Mental Health Unit and in nursing education:

1. The framework of the project was used as the basis for a model ward training project (see Chapter 8);
2. The Sisters' Group continued to be a forum for discussion;

3. The Health Authority built on the experiences of Bill Lemmer as in-service training officer to propose and provide funding for a nursing development adviser, who built on the values and principles of the project (see Chapter 8);
4. Two of the collaborators got together to disseminate the work through articles, presentations, and the present book.

6.12 SUMMING UP AND CONCLUSION

Although there were many questions asked at the beginning of this project, and during it, it seems appropriate to start this summary with an answer to the central question.

The project through its developing and changing educational input into these five wards was successful in bringing about changes, i.e. changes in people's attitudes and perceptions, together with changes in approaches to care; and although not formally evaluated, we would argue that the result was an improvement in patient care. We can conclude many other things from the project in addition to demonstrating that our approach to facilitating change has worked; we present some of the specific conclusions here, although this whole book is a testament to the things we have learnt.

1. *Questioning and evaluation.* Clearly, both these have been of central importance in the project. We would advocate them as a central part of any education intervention. Within our own health authority educationalists are beginning to address the question we sought to answer, namely; 'what effect, if any, is this intervention having?'
2. *Groupwork.* A cornerstone of our work was allowing people to pool their resources and benefit from each other's skills. It helped develop teamwork and continuity within the wards with an undoubted benefit to staff and patients;
3. *Collaboration.* The value of getting managers, teachers, researchers, specialists, and practitioners together has enhanced everyone's work and helped all to pull in the same direction. With approaching change in the field of mental health, we think this is a crucial factor in their success;
4. *Action research framework.* We believe that this approach has been

central to the success of the project. In research terms we have overcome many of Hunt's (1981) problems with nursing research through using this framework. The benefits of sharing data and participation are there for all to see;

5. *Pace of change.* Each stage of this project has further confirmed our view that change, if it is to include those people already *in situ*, needs to proceed at a careful pace. Necessity dictates that this is a slow pace, interspersed with continual checking out of the views of the people involved. The alternative of losing the people in the area and introducing new people leaves behind many casualties. Currently this difficult choice faces many managers in mental health;
6. *Resource implications.* We believe that the resources of people, time, and energy invested in this three-year project were more than outweighed by the benefits. However, it is necessary to record that facilitating change does bear a cost. When people talk about introducing change, then they must be aware of the resources required.

It must be obvious that we, and the project steering group, think our efforts have been worthwhile. But perhaps that is not enough. The need for change had been clearly brought home to our particular health authority by a visit and report of the Hospital Advisory Service (1986). The information was already there for all to see in the data we collected and reported on. However, it perhaps takes an outside, powerful body to shift the inertia of a large institution. The model we developed for facilitating change was taken on and suggested within a model ward project (see Chapter 7) — an indication of the success of the project.

Perhaps the success of the project is captured in the following diary entries:

> 'Patients were sitting in groups. One patient joined us at the team meeting.'
>
> 'Nurses and patients seem more expressive. . .joined at our talk by two different patients.'
>
> 'There was a feeling of ease and accomplishment in the ward team.'
>
> 'Patients talking to each other.'
>
> 'Nursing assistants talked about playing draughts with patients, reading newspapers with them, allowing them to choose their own clothing.'

'Four patients who were 'noisy and disruptive' usually sit in psychiatric chairs. . .have been grouped around a table. Their chairs are not in a tipped back position and they look much more alert.'

REFERENCES

Fretwell, J.E. (1982) *Ward Training and Learning*, RCN, London.

Greenwood, J. (1984) Nursing research: a position paper. *Journal of Advanced Nursing*, **9**, 77–82.

Hospital Advisory Service (1986) *Report of a Visit to a South London Hospital*, HAS, Beckenham.

Hunt, J. (1981) Indicators for nursing practice: the use of research findings. *Journal of Advanced Nursing*, **6**, 180–94.

Kitson, A.L. (1985) *Therapeutic Nursing Function of the Ward Sister*, Proceeding of the Twenty-fifth Research Society Conference, RCN, London.

Lathleen, J. and Farnish, S. (1984) *The Ward Sister Training Project*. Nursing Education Research Unit Report No. 3, King's College, University of London.

Martin, J.P. (1984) *Hospitals in Trouble*, Blackwell, Oxford.

Walker, R. (1980) The conduct of educational case studies: ethics, theory and procedures, in W.B. Dockrell and D. Hamilton (eds) *Rethinking Educational Research*, Hodder and Stoughton, London.

Walton, H. (ed.) (1971) *Small Group Psychotherapy*, Penguin, Harmondsworth.

APPENDIX A: QUESTIONNAIRE FOR TOOTING BEC HOSPITAL

No: ______________

Thank you for completing this questionnaire. Your replies will be confidential and anonymous. None of your responses will be attributed directly to you.

There are no right or wrong answers. Please answer the questions as honestly and fully as possible. The questionnaire is designed to get an impression of how you feel about your job.

The aim of the questionnaire is to help us make a suitable training plan for your ward. We will give you the questionnaire a few times over a six-month trial period, so that we can see how things have changed.

If you have any difficulty in completing this questionnaire or would like some help to fill it in, please contact: – Mr Bill Lemmer or Mrs K. McClafferty – just ask the hospital telephone operator to bleep.

It is important to answer the questions yourself as it is your views we want. When answering questions please:

1. Tick correct box (example): (Ignore numbers in the boxes)

   Yes [✓ 1]

   No [2]

2. You may place your cross (x) anywhere on the line. The cross will mark where your feelings lie:

   (example)

   Happy —x———————————— Unhappy

INTRODUCTION

1. What grade of staff are you:

   Sister/Charge Nurse [1]

   Staff Nurse [2]

   Enrolled nurse [3]

   Learner nurse [4]

   Assistant nurse [5]

2. Do you work:

full-time [1]

or

part-time [2]

3. How long have you worked at Tooting Bec Hospital:

less than 6 months [1]

more than 6 months but less than 1 year [2]

more than 1 year but less than 5 years [3]

more than 5 years but less than 10 years [4]

more than 10 years [5]

4. Question deleted.

ALLOCATION

5. What type of ward are you working on? ______________________

6. Did you choose to work on this particular ward:

Yes [1]

No [2]

7. Do you allocate, or assign, the work to other nurses:

Yes [1]

No [2]

8. How is the nurses' work allocated on your ward:

by having patients to look after [ ] 1

by having areas of the ward to look after [ ] 2

by having jobs to do [ ] 3

by everyone doing everything [ ] 4

combination of the above, or other (please specify) [ ] 5

____

9. Does this method of nurse allocation:

work well [ ] 1

work alright [ ] 2

not work well [ ] 3

not work [ ] 4

10. Do you have a choice in which patients you look after:

Yes [ ] 1

No [ ] 2

11. Is the allocation of work each shift generally:
(please mark with a cross (x) at the appropriate point on the line)

unfair |———————————————| fair

too much |———————————————| too little

12. Do you usually work:

harder than other nurses	1
about the same as other nurses	2
less hard than other nurses	3

13. Are there other nurses on your ward who:

	Yes	*No*
work harder than you	1	2
work less hard than you	1	2

14. Is the number of staff provided adequate to give *all* the nursing care that you would want to give:

Yes	1
No	2
Don't know	9

15. Is the number of staff provided adequate to give *all* the basic nursing care:

Yes	1
No	2
Don't know	9

16. Do you get the same set of patients to look after:

all the time [ ] 1

some of the time [ ] 2

only occasionally [ ] 3

never [ ] 4

it varies the whole time [ ] 5

PATIENTS

17. How many patients are there on the ward:
(please fill in with a number)

to-day [ ][ ]

when full [ ][ ]

don't know [ ]

18. How many patients are new to the ward in the last 7 days:

Please state number [ ][ ]

Don't know [ ][ ]

19. How do you address your patients:

By first name [ ] 1

By title and surname [2]

By nickname [3]

By whatever they like [4]

Combination of above, or other [5]

20. How often do you talk to other nurses on the ward about patients:

Frequently [1]

Occasionally [2]

Rarely [3]

Never [4]

21. Do patients ever.

	Yes	*No*
frighten you	1	2
worry you	1	2
pester you	1	2
swear at you	1	2
thank you	1	2

22. Do you think that the care you give your patients is helping them to return to the community?

Yes	1
No	2
Don't know	9

23. Which aspect of your care do you think your patients enjoy the most?

24. Which aspect of your care do you most enjoy doing?

25. Which *one* of the following statements *best* describes your work with patients:

Treating them like a member of the family	1
Keeping them clean, comfortable and tidy whilst they are ill	2
Rehabilitating them for life in the community	3
Helping to protect their individuality and maintain independence	4
None of these	5

26. Do patients have their own individual belongings on the ward

	Yes	*No*
furniture	1	2
clothes	1	2

toiletries	1	2
jewellery	1	2
other	1	2

please specify: ________

27. How many of the patients – on the ward – do you think will eventually get out into the community:

all	1
most	2
some	3
none	4

ORGANIZATION OF WORK

28. Is the work on the ward:

well organized |————————————————| badly organized

29. Are you in your own work:

well organized |————————————————| badly organized

30. When do the following patient activities take place: (please tick one box for each activity.)

	Set time(s)	*Any time*	*Both*
getting up	1	2	3

washing/bathing	1	2	3
bedmaking	1	2	3
exercise	1	2	3
drinks (tea/coffee)	1	2	3
occupational therapy	1	2	3
lunch	1	2	3
dressings	1	2	3
doctors' rounds	1	2	3
visiting within the ward	1	2	3
trips away from the ward	1	2	3
recreational therapy	1	2	3

31. Is the patient's day:

Organized much the same each day	1
Varies each day	2

32. Are there jobs around the ward that you have to do on a regular basis:

	each shift	*daily*	*weekly*	*occas-ionally*	*never*
cleaning	1	2	3	4	5
tidying	1	2	3	4	5
stocking up	1	2	3	4	5
ordering	1	2	3	4	5
teaching	1	2	3	4	5

33. If you had the power, is there anything you would change about the work:

Yes 1

No 2

If 'Yes' (to question 33) please say what:

ROLES

34. Is your role/job description written down on paper:

Yes 1

No 2

35. Have you a copy of your role/job description:

Yes	1
No	2

36. Who decides what your role is:

District Committee	1
Senior Nurse	2
Sister	3
Qualified Nurse	4
Me	5
None of above	6

37. Are you satisfied with your role:

Yes	1
No	2

How satisfied:

Very satisfied ———————————————— Very dissatisfied

38. Would you like to have more choice in deciding your role:

Yes	1
No	2

39. Which of the following activities do you include in your role. (Please tick either Yes or No)

	Yes	*No*
Talking to patients	1	2
Admitting patients	1	2
Giving drugs	1	2
Talking to relatives	1	2
Writing Kardex	1	2
Incontinence care	1	2
Bathing	1	2
Bed making	1	2
Dressings	1	2
Observations (B/P)	1	2
Feeding patients	1	2
Assessing patients' needs	1	2

40. Question deleted.

41. Is there any confusion about your own role?

Yes [1]

No [2]

TRAINING

42. Have you any nursing qualifications:

Yes [1]

No [2]

If 'Yes', which:

SRN (RGN) [1]

RMN [2]

SEN [3]

SEN (M) [4]

SEN (G) [5]

Doubly qualified [6]

43. Have you received any specific training for the job you do now:

Yes [1]

No [2]

If 'Yes', what form did it take?

study day	1
2–3 study days	2
several study days	3
study week	4
2 or more study weeks	5
study afternoons	6

Was it part of your orientation:

Yes	1
No	2

44. Do you think you need specific training for your job:

Yes	1
No	2

If 'Yes', where should it take place:

on wards	1
in school	2
outside	3
combination of the above, or other	4

Who should train you:

ward staff	☐	1
senior nurse	☐	2
tutors	☐	3
outside trainers	☐	4
combination of the above	☐	5

45. What sort of things have you learnt in this present job:

SUPERVISION

46. Are you supervised in your work:

Yes	☐	1
No	☐	2

If 'Yes', who supervises you:

Senior Nurse	☐	3
Sister/Charge Nurse	☐	4
Qualified Nurse	☐	5
Two or more of the above	☐	6

Is this supervision:

Very helpful |————————————————| Unhelpful

Constructive |————————————————| Destructive

47. Who do you think should supervise your work:

Senior Nurse	1
Sister/Charge Nurse	2
Qualified Nurse	3
No one	4
Two or more of the above	5

48. Do you decide what tasks to do:

Yes	1
No	2

ACCOUNTABILITY

49. Who is responsible for the safety of patients on your ward:

Senior Nurse	1
Sister/Charge Nurse	2
Qualified nurse	3
Person looking after patient	4
Whole team	5
Other ____________	6

50. Who is responsible for the nursing care of patients on your ward:

Senior Nurse	1
Sister/Charge Nurse	2
Qualified nurse	3
Person looking after patient	4
Whole team	5
Other ________________	6

51. If you made a serious mistake on the ward, who would you tell first:

____

PLANNING

52. How do you decide to do the following things:

	My own decision	*When I'm told to*	*Not at all*
Give drugs	1	2	3
Do dressings	1	2	3
Talk to patients	1	2	3
Bath patients	1	2	3
Walk with patients	1	2	3

Write Kardex	1	2	3
Put patients at ease	1	2	3
Socialize with patients	1	2	3

53. Do you have to tell other nurses what to do: Yes 1 No 2

54. Does anyone tell you what to do: Yes 1 No 2

55. Should anyone tell you what to do: Yes 1 No 2

56. Is there a handover between shifts: Yes 1 No 2

(a) If there is a handover, how long is it usually:

	less than 10 mins	*15 mins*	*20 mins*	*25 mins*	*more than 30 mins*
between day shifts	1	2	3	4	5
between day/night	1	2	3	4	5
between night/day	1	2	3	4	5

(b) Who attends handover:

Sister/Charge Nurse only	1
Qualified nurses only	2
Nursing Assistants only	3
Everyone	4

(c) At handover, do you talk about:

	all patients	*some patients*	*very few patients*
between day shifts	1	2	3
between day/night	1	2	3
between night/day	1	2	3

(d) Do you usually say something at handover:

Yes	1
No	2

57. How often is the nursing care of each patient on your ward reviewed:

once a shift or more	1
at handover	2
each day	3
each week	4

monthly [5]

whenever patient needs it [6]

never [7]

58. How often do you think the care of each patient on your ward should be reviewed:

once a shift or more [1]

at handover [2]

each day [3]

each week [4]

monthly [5]

whenever patients needs it [6]

never [7]

59. Are you involved in planning the care of your patients:

Yes [1]

No [2]

60. Do you ever write down in the various notes: *Yes* *No*

Patient care [1] [2]

Patient's routine [1] [2]

Patient's assessment [1] [2]

61 Do you admit patients to the ward:

Yes [1]

No [2]

COMMUNICATION

62. Do other members of the nursing staff listen to what you have to say:

All the time [1]

Most of the time [2]

Some of the time [3]

Never [4]

63. Do Nurse Managers (Senior Nurses) listen to what you have to say:

All the time [1]

Most of the time [2]

Some of the time [3]

Never [4]

64. Do doctors listen to what you have to say:

All the time [1]

Most of the time [2]

Some of the time [3]

Never [4]

Not applicable [5]

65. How do you find out what has happened to patients when you are first on duty:

From being told [1]

From reading notes [2]

From the patient [3]

Don't find out [4]

Two or more of the above [5]

66. If you are sent to work on another ward, how do you find out about the patients:

From being told [1]

From reading notes [2]

From the patient [3]

Don't find out [4]

I never work away from my ward [ ] 5

Two or more of the above [ ] 6

67. Have you ever refused to do a task because of lack of communication:

Yes [ ] 1

No [ ] 2

If yes, please say what it was: ______________________________

68. Are you satisfied with the communications between shifts:

Yes [ ] 1

No [ ] 2

69. Are you satisfied with the communication between nurses:

Yes [ ] 1

No [ ] 2

70. Do you think you need more communication skills:

Yes [ ] 1

No [ ] 2

71. Is there adequate communication between patients:

Yes [ ] 1

No [ ] 2

YOU AND YOUR WORK

72. How do you feel about your work:

Happy	|——————| Unhappy
Very interested	|——————| Very bored
Easy	|——————| Too much pressure
No worries	|——————| Very worried
Full of energy	|——————| Very tired
Stimulated	|——————| Very repetitive

73. Which one of the following statements do you agree with most strongly:

(a) I'm here to do the work; one shift is much the same as another. ☐ 1

(b) The work changes from shift to shift, depending on who is working. ☐ 2

(c) The work depends on how the patients are; it's worse when they're restless. ☐ 3

(d) The work is the same each shift, but you get out of it what you put into it. ☐ 4

(e) The work of a shift depends on how nurses assess the needs of the patients. ☐ 5

74. Does the work affect your family or those you are close to:

Yes ☐ 1

No ☐ 2

If 'Yes', in what way: ____________________

75. In the work that you do are you:

Tired all the time ☐ 1

Tired towards the end of a shift ☐ 2

Tired after a few hours of duty ☐ 3

Never tired ☐ 4

Mentally but not physically tired ☐ 5

Combination of the above ☐ 6

76. Are there days when you just don't feel like coming to work:

Frequently ☐ 1

Occasionally ☐ 2

Never ☐ 3

77. If you felt unwell, would you:

Come in and work the whole shift ☐ 1

Come in and see how it went ☐ 2

Take a day off to recover ☐ 3

Talk to the boss about it ☐ 4

Combination of the above ☐ 5

78. What sort of things make it worth coming to work:

....

....

....

....

79. What puts you off coming to work:

....

....

....

....

ENVIRONMENT

80. Is the ward:

Bright	├──────────┤	Dull
Clean	├──────────┤	Dirty
Too spacious	├──────────┤	Too cramped
Well laid out	├──────────┤	Poorly laid out
Well decorated	├──────────┤	Poorly decorated
Well equipped	├──────────┤	Poorly equipped
Homely	├──────────┤	Unfriendly

81. Have you any ideas for improving the ward:

....

....

....

....

82. Do the patients have adequate privacy: Yes [1] No [2]

GENERAL

These questions will help us understand the wards better and help in designing the most appropriate training programme. This information will, of course, be treated confidentially.

83. Your age:

18–24	1
25–29	2
30–39	3
40–49	4
Over 50	5

84. Sex:

Female	1
Male	2

85. Your birthplace is:

Outside UK	*Inside UK*
1	2

86. Ethnic origin:

African	1
Greek	2
Bangladeshi	3
Irish	4
Chinese	5

West Indian [ ] 6

Mauritian [ ] 7

Filipino [ ] 8

Other [ ]

(please specify)________

Thank you for completing this questionnaire. We hope you have enjoyed filling it in. Are there any comments you would like to make?

APPENDIX B: CHANGES INDICATED BY THE DIARIES

Date	*Ward*	*Entry*
15/2/85	1	Nurses genuinely concerned about doing what was right.
18/2/85	5	Changes in ward environment, e.g. more homely arrangement of chairs and tables, large sign over dormitory door: 'Smile you're in ward 5.
20/2/85	4	Began to discuss more issues around patient care, more patient concerns raised. Staff using ward diary to communicate details of meeting.
4/3/85	5	Good team contribution.
8/3/85	4	Concern expressed by staff about lack of curtains in wash basin area, so no privacy. Staff welcoming and spontaneous.
11/3/85	5	The physical environment of the ward is even more dramatically changed this week, and the nurses seemed to think they and the patients were pleased. Patients were sitting in three groups: one patient joined us at the team meeting. . . Still more calendar and orientation posters were up and all the dormitory lockers and beds were comfortably arranged with each locker adorned with name, personal items, and cards.
11/3/85	3	One of the staff pointed out the importance of maintaining some flexibility and changing as situations demanded.
13/3/85	4	Nurses responsible for ordering toiletries, menu choices, and seeing to general clothing needs of their allocated patients. Some expressed pleasure in being able to do this.
18/3/85	5	Twelve new lounger chairs on ward, 6 less geriatric chairs, and only 5 left (24-bed ward). Nurses involved in individual assessments. Nurses and patients are brighter, although the nurses seem to undervalue their achievement. Nurses and patients seem more expressive. . .joined at our talk by two different patients.
19/3/85	2	Reported success with daily supervision and toilet programme and contact.
20/3/85	4	New curtains in ward.

26/3/85	2	There was a feeling of ease and accomplishment in the ward team. Indeed they had returned two patients to the community and nursed three others to a position of 'trial leave'. They related how – by supervision and just being there – a patient was helped into an acceptable toilet routine.
1/4/85	5	It felt as though a good deal of participation took place in the meeting and that there was a little more focus on patients' problems.
3/4/85	2	An enthusiastic handover by sister followed by a very lively and animated discussion.
8/4/85	5	Report from sister contained items related to individual care, indicates that problem-solving thinking had occurred.
9/4/85	1	Interesting handover from each group nurse focusing on patients' problems. A lady who was 'screaming' stopped last Thursday, apparently due to administering drugs which eased pain in her hip joint.
10/4/85	4	Patients talking to each other. Each nurse discussed group of patients without prompting. Individual care issues discussed. NAs talked about playing draughts with patients, reading newspapers with them, allowing them to choose own clothing. It was evident that nurses had been taking a special interest in their patients.
15/4/85	5	The ward has made a three-foot-square individualized care plan board that hangs in office, and it lists and illustrates the enormous effort made by the nurses. I could not praise them enough.
16/4/85	1	It was good to hear nurses giving argument to their views.
17/4/85	4	On entering the ward, the staff were actively involved with patients and showed spontaneous signs of affection towards them. Ward looked tidy and organized. TV turned off. Team work evident.
24/4/85	4	Nurses taking a pride in their patients. Timetable on walls of meal times as part of reality orientation. Calendar moved lower down the wall, so that patients could change date. Teamwork improved.
29/4/85	1	Always an interesting and keen session with this

		active and well-motivated team.
1/5/85	4	The staff were all pleased that I had come to meeting and were most anxious to show me how many changes they had made in the bed area and sitting area. The ward did indeed look good.
1/5/85	2	They were bursting with things to say.
6/5/85	5	This is the first time that a ward team has actively used a team meeting to do care planning with existing documentation.
8/5/85	4	Staff *much* more imaginative in their thinking and approach to patient problems. TV programmes being watched and discussed with patients. Old songs being sung! Positive attitude and sense of humour prevail.
15/5/85	4	The ward layout had been changed. One patient usually sits talking to the mirror...she now sits with the group of ladies and is not talking to the mirror as much. Four patients who were 'noisy and disruptive' usually sit in psychogeriatric chairs, have been grouped round a table. Their chairs are not in tipped-back position and they look much more alert.
15/5/85	2	Team seemed bubbling with enthusiasm and initiative.
22/5/85	4	Two patients transferred out because of progress made.
27/5/85	5	Veronica and others out of geriatric chairs – leaving only one person.
29/5/85	4	Communication within team developing well. All patients looked well-dressed and tended to. Visitors to ward well received.
13/6/85	4	Staff expressed considerable concern about patients who had progressed in the ward and been transferred for rehabilitation and then deteriorating. Wondered if effort was worth anything? The staff on the ward are showing signs of beginning to identify what is an acceptable standard of care and the need to provide continuity of care.
17/8/85	5	Generally all evaluations showed patients progressing with their care plans although measured with

		subjective criteria...clearly communicated with team.
26/8/85	4	Although previous comments had been that meetings hadn't changed things, people then started to say that this [project] would help more wards breach their standard!
8/9/85	5	Patients quite spirited today, a tribute, I speculate, to the nurses' ability to stimulate and orientate the people in their care. Acknowledged personal and professional growth in the team.

APPENDIX C: THE DIFFICULTIES INDICATED BY THE DIARIES

Date	*Ward*	*Entry*
11/2/85	5	EN'S example of cultural difficulties: not looking directly into patient's eyes.
12/2/85	2	There's nothing you can do for patients [these ones] . . . they're all going downhill.
13/2/85	1	Mrs X – smeared herself with a smelly stool.
15/2/85	4	Nurse required to work on another ward. Usual noisy morning, quiet morning, no problems.
18/2/85	5	EN said it was not possible to provide psychological care under the pressure of tasks. Last week's goal was not done.
18/2/85	3	Report centred around physical care. Problems of patients having wool strip tied across the arms of their chairs to prevent them standing and falling.
19/2/85	2	Meeting did not start till 2.05 (due to start 1.30 and sister wanted to leave at 2.20). Descriptions of patients 'going down'; don't trust us; resistive; crying; incontinent.
20/2/85	4	Needed to slow down as tended to speed through and not allow people to expand their feelings about patients; concerned about appearance of ward but staff felt it was hopeless . . .
25/2/85	5	Orientation board day/date was not correct again, but it was not appropriate to mention this as there was an immediate conflict between sister and staff.
26/2/85	2	'You can't look after patients if the team isn't here to do it.' Two new nurses booked in . . . did not know if a patient had, say, the right slippers and clothing. Disagreement between shifts about where the chairs are and what patients wear.
27/2/85	4	Some surprise expressed that patients were actually aware.
27/2/85	1	Heated exchanges between sister and senior nurse. I [facilitator] was quite worried about the nurse managers' ability to participate in change when we are still clearly, in a phase of developing trust, understanding and defining our goals.

4/3/85	5	Report was a subjective and generalized account: 'going down', 'down under the weather', 'very, very incontinent', 'restless and agitated'. [Bill] You tell us what to do.
4/3/85	3	Impossible to implement [nursing process] because they didn't have enough staff.
5/3/85	2	No agreement on care.
6/3/85	1	Twelve of 19 patients on 20 points (NS)
8/3/85	4	All [patients] washed and dressed by 8.30 a.m. as later on nurses had to run errands and put away laundry.
11/3/85	3	Couldn't carry out psychological care. Discussed how staff could fight the system, e.g. wearing jewellery. One of the more senior nurses said that junior staff did not pay the senior staff any respect. In reply to this, one of the juniors said they were treated like children by the seniors.
13/3/85	4	Discussed the problems of one lady being disruptive – staff felt it was impossible to do anything with her, one even said that there was no point in assessing her.
13/3/85	4	Open disapproval expressed (of getting patients up to breakfast in dressing-gowns).
13/3/85	1	Nurses dealing with difficult behavioural problem.
16/3/85	3	Staff said they became ill because they worked too hard. Did not seem to be using equipment. Staff began to talk about how angry some of the patients made them.
17/3/85	5	Pads being sat on instead of being worn. Long discussion on nurses' conflict with patients.
18/3/85	5	'No change generally', 'no immediate complaints' 'restless and agitated', 'pleasant and co-operative', 'apprehensive about patients' self-care'.
20/5/85	4	Issue of social prejudice discussed. Patient doesn't like blacks. Lack of continuity and communication between two shifts highlighted.
20/5/85	1	Great deal of anxiety in meeting.
25/5/85	3	Couldn't do 'therapy' because they were short-staffed.

26/3/85	2	Day nurses' entire pattern of working with the patients as individuals is upset Sunday–Tuesday nights because a night nursing team's routine did not allow people to get up prior to the day staff coming on duty.
27/3/85	4	Ward very noisy and patients very restless. When I mentioned it to the nurses, they said it was the weather or a full moon. The TV is always on, nurses were shouting at patients and laughing at some of the behaviour.
1/4/85	3	One of the nurses...felt we repeated similar things each week...she went on to say that patients never change, so they would provide us with little to talk about...Ward 3 so boring.
1/4/85	4	No attempt by sister to allow nurses to discuss their individual groups of patients.
6/4/85	3	Nothing wrong with their present level of nursing care and that standards would go down if the nursing process was implemented.
25/4/85	3	Found only one shift working in an individualized way.
29/4/85	3	It was explained that maybe the group was unsafe to talk in.
1/5/85	4	I felt there was a lack of understanding on the nursing process.
1/5/85	2	A member of the night staff is reportedly taking off all incontinence pads which the day staff use in patient care. It was mentioned that night staff threatened not to take over the ward unless patients were in bed and did not care for the patients, in some cases, in the mornings.
6/5/85	5	However, it became clear that nurses were uncertain about what to do (rewriting care plans).
7/5/85	2	Nurses not prepared, senior nurses not told either word (about change in day).
8/5/85	1	A rather casual meeting, little focus on individualized care.
10/5/85	3	Group lacked enthusiasm.
13/5/85	5	I put it to the nurses that I was worried about their

		not accepting responsibility for their work. The team seemed depressed.
15/5/85	2	Difficulties were reported between nurses and visitors over reporting patients as violent.
20/5/85	5	Very subdued ward team, patients also subdued, nobody would say.
22/5/85	4	Staff attributed an accident directly to allowing patient more freedom. Distressed by accident.
22/5/85	2	Talk of people not pulling weight.
28/5/85	1	Nurses exasperated with two ladies, one throwing things and hitting all the nurses and the other was scratching and barely approachable.
29/5/85	2	Such was impact of discussion, EN giving injection, sister walking about, two NAs struggling with patient in kitchen, one NA watching TV. Formal patient complaint last week and sister particularly feeling strain.
3/6/85	5	EN didn't speak for whole hour – no apparent reason.
13/6/85	4	Not always easy for staff to grasp that patients will respond to explanations.
20/6/85	2	Nurses spoke quite harshly about the allocation not working on one shift. Someone mentioned patient being neglected – nurses said they were overstretched. Nurses being neglected, too. Negative view of themselves.
26/6/85	2	Meeting disrupted by nurses getting up and leaving without saying a word. Hostile feeling expressed to new care plans.
26/6/85	4	'Nothing has changed.' Feel that ward has reached a plateau and is in need of a break in August/September/October.
1/7/85	4	As at beginning of this project, staff have difficulty in implementing appropriate nursing action for patients who are physically unwell and need considerable help and guidance on this.
1/7/85	3	I said I felt that I hadn't helped them to create a

		group that was safe enough for them to discuss their relationships.
15/7/85	3	The group finished with the observation being made that many members of the group appeared afraid of living with anger and rejection.
16/7/85	1	Nurses at all levels resented they were not taken notice of.

— 7 —
Changing structure

How the Management of Change Project decided *what* to change, *why* 'structural' change was necessary, *who* was involved, and *what* happened – these questions are the subjects of this chapter, together with examples of structural changes. The reader may wish to thumb through the following pages in order to gain an overview of what is going to be discussed. However, the chapter begins to develop the perspective of changing structure by addressing our terms of reference, e.g. change, structure, and the flow of events.

First, deciding what to change meant evaluating, as a way of valuing, what already existed. What we brought to the project was a strong personal commitment to enquiry and discovery as ways of participating with colleagues and clients. So while there are a number of definitions, and the like, to be considered, all are flavoured with the taste of working with people where they are at.

A definition of evaluation in nursing includes making judgements about the degree of success in meeting goals. Hence 'The nurse evaluates effects of measures used, the need for *change* in goals of care, the accuracy of the implementation of nursing, and the need for *change* in the client's environment' (Urdang and Swallow, 1983, p. 402). This is, of course, an evaluation in the context of the nursing process. When what is wanted in the first place is compared with the actual outcome a measure of effectiveness is thus obtained.

Therefore, the nursing process can be described as a sort of 'rolling cycle', approach to the way that nurses intervene in patient or client care. Making changes in the way the nursing is provided may occur as the care moves along, and reassessing therefore becomes a part of evaluation, even before a final outcome is established.

Clark (1983) refers to evaluation when a person assesses something on the merits of its value; three dimensions of this evaluation are:

1. based upon a person's perception – evaluation is subjective;
2. based upon an object, say, a ward – how would it be described?
3. based upon different values – how is good value distinguished from poor value?

Evaluation is portrayed in Fig. 7.1 as part of an interactive process. Referring to the definitions of the term evaluation, this process, for nurses, is multi-dimensional, in so far as we would be interacting with our environment on the ward as well as with the people who are there. Therefore, as discussed in Chapter 2, we are involved in the change as thinking, feeling, and doing participants.

The use of a process method (the nursing process) as a structure for delivery of services is intended to ensure individualized, client-centred care. A change in structure alone will not work unless people who use it have preparation before the change and support when the change is implemented. For example, during the five-ward Project, hospital management decided that a new nursing process format would be used, starting on a particular day. In the Project group work, it became clear that the new format structure was unusable. These forms carried with them assumptions that people had understood, experienced and agreed the kind of actions and attitudes expected by managers to be written down, never mind expecting what was written to reflect what happens on the wards. Nursing which is provided with a process method should be undertaken in terms of structure, process, and client outcome (World Health Organization, 1979).

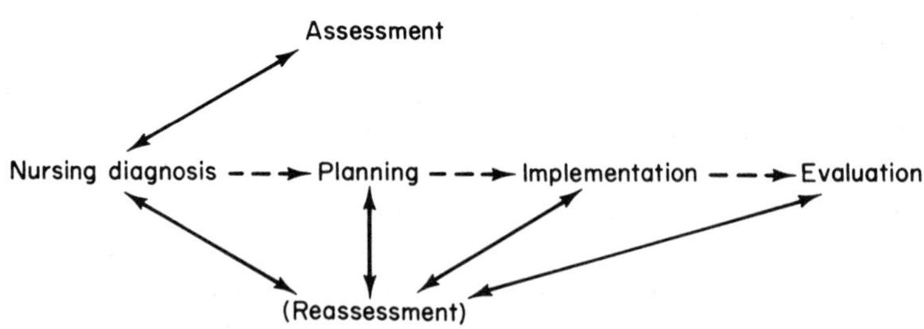

Fig. 7.1 The nursing process (from George, 1985).

How to decide about what to change, why change the way people work, who is involved, how to evaluate what happens? – these questions about the quality and effectiveness of nursing care occur alongside the trend towards professional accountability and the rise in consumer expectations. Also rising costs in health care further amplify the question of how effective is the care given to clients and how effective is the practice of nursing. Altschul considers the nursing implications of the consumer's voice:

> We want to enable the patient in hospital to live as nearly as possible to the way he does at home...if only we can arrive at the right theoretical formulation...the patient's needs will become manifest.
>
> (Altschul, 1983, pp. 175–83)

A useful framework for evaluating what is the right approach has been developed by Donabedian (1966, 1969). He suggests that three components be considered in evaluating the quality of health care; and each of these components requires its own approach and methods. The three components are structure, process, and outcome. In Fig. 7.2 we illustrate the three approaches to evaluation in a framework which is underpinned by a process method of nursing.

Now we turn to what is structure. The structure part of the evaluative framework includes all the factors associated with the care setting: the physical facilities, equipment, staffing levels, organizational structure, characteristics of care givers, and even the kinds of form used for recording and documenting nursing care.

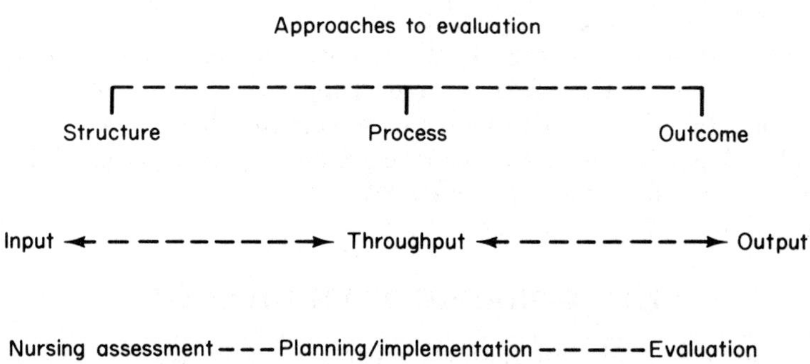

Fig. 7.2 Donabedian framework for evaluating quality.

Process refers to the performance of care givers, and in particular what the nurse does and how she does it: this comprises the action and meaning of the nursing process. Outcome is the result of care, defined in terms of the client's condition and welfare.

The Nodder Committee (1980) has recommended a method of structural evaluation for the organization and management problems of mental hospitals. It is a management audit designed to check that standards of patient care are kept at a reasonable level. It is intended that in looking at the structure of a ward, say, the kind of incident or behaviour or malpractice that can lead to an injury might be avoided. The Nodder Report provides one method of looking at structure only; it includes as appendices a draft standards document, and a checklist, reproduced from a similar report on standards of care for the mentally ill and mentally handicapped in Wales (Nodder, 1980, Appendices D and E). This document covers patients' activities, rehabilitation, recreation, privacy, personal clothes and possessions, noise, visiting, lights-out, accessibility to toilets, heating, laundering, decoration, and repair of living accommodation as well as staffing ratios, bed space, and ward furniture.

The structural approach, unrelated to the process and outcome dimensions of evaluation, will have little, if any, value, either to the patients, the nurses, or to the organization. A structural evaluation is an inappropriate measure for the effectiveness of nursing care. The strengths of a structural approach to evaluation lie in mustering concrete and accessible information which should be easy to obtain. The weakness of structural evaluation lies in its basic assumption: if the structure is good, good care will follow; if the quantity is right, quality will follow.

Evaluation and changes in the area of nursing structure should be consistent with evaluation and changes in the process area of nursing (process evaluation is the subject of Chapters 4, 5, 6, 8, and 9); Figs. 7.3 and 7.4 illustrate examples of measures in all three areas of the Donabedian framework.

7.1 WORKING WITH CHANGE

Before considering actual structural changes in the Management of Change Project, we need to examine change as a term of reference

Approaches to Evaluation

Structure	Process	Outcome
Nodder audit	Qualpacs	Phaneuf audit
GNC nurse training hospitals criteria	Monitor	Health status indexes
Job performance review	Process recording	
Peer review		
(Indicate the aims and purposes of institutions, agencies, or programmes).	(Used in evaluation of actions and the sequence of behaviours and events during care delivery)	(Developed to evaluate the end-result of care and service provided)

Fig. 7.3 Methods of evaluating quality discussed in the Donabedian framework.

Approaches to evaluation

Structure	Process	Outcome
Job performance review, leading to identification of ward manager's training needs	Action research tools: critical incident questionnaires; participant observer accounts of staff support groups (ward teams).	Criteria to be formulated
Steering Group	Tooting Bec Hospital 86-item questionnaire.	Providing baseline quality appraisal
Peer review		

Fig. 7.4 Development of the current project in the evaluation framework.

for our study (see also Chapter 6). Today's demands upon psychiatric nursing are not necessarily consistent with the way nursing practice developed over many years (Chapter 1). The process of nursing and the evaluation of quality care tend to be described in terms of a system – i.e. in terms of systems theory. The nursing process is usually referred to as a problem-solving system. Nursing is often said to be systematic. Psychiatric nursing is an interpersonal and helping service; it is action-oriented. The development of relationships and the way in which those relations are useful to clients is not necessarily systematic.

Thus the tradition of mental nursing and the professionalizing demands of contemporary nursing as a whole are not completely consistent with psychiatric nursing today. This means that today's nursing practitioners in mental health care face changes which arise out of the past in terms of custodial care, and which also arise out of the present in terms of translating professional accountability and process nursing into interpersonal care. Change, then, impacts with the past and present. Psychiatric nursing has its own identity to find. Coupled with this, a third aspect of change is the internal change in each nurse which is associated with growing, developing as a person, and learning (Chapter 2). Given the traditional, professional, and personal aspects of change, we might wish to add a fourth dimension to the Donabedian framework (Fig. 7.2): the well-being of the nurse.

The principal energies in psychiatric nursing may come from within and from outside the relationships between individual nurses and their clients. This is an important consideration in approaching evaluation and in considering how education, management, and nursing practice can be used to inform and enhance and support the care.

In Fig. 7.5 a systems diagram is used to illustrate the collaborative process to make changes. This is a bringing together of structure, process, and outcome (note that different methods are used for different parts of the evaluative process – Figs 7.3 and 7.4). The circles in Fig. 7.5 represent the participant systems of the change process, namely nursing management, nursing education, and nursing practice including the elderly clients. The systems have subsystems, each with their status and functions, for example, the linen and the whole business of maintaining an individual wardrobe of dresses. Suprasystems outside the circles include, for instance, the National Health Service and the Department of Health and Social Security. The focus of the model in Fig. 7.5 is the intersystem, where the collaboration of nursing, education, and management takes place. This model highlights the intention of the Management of Change Project that desired change is not conceived or planned or instituted by outsiders of one system or

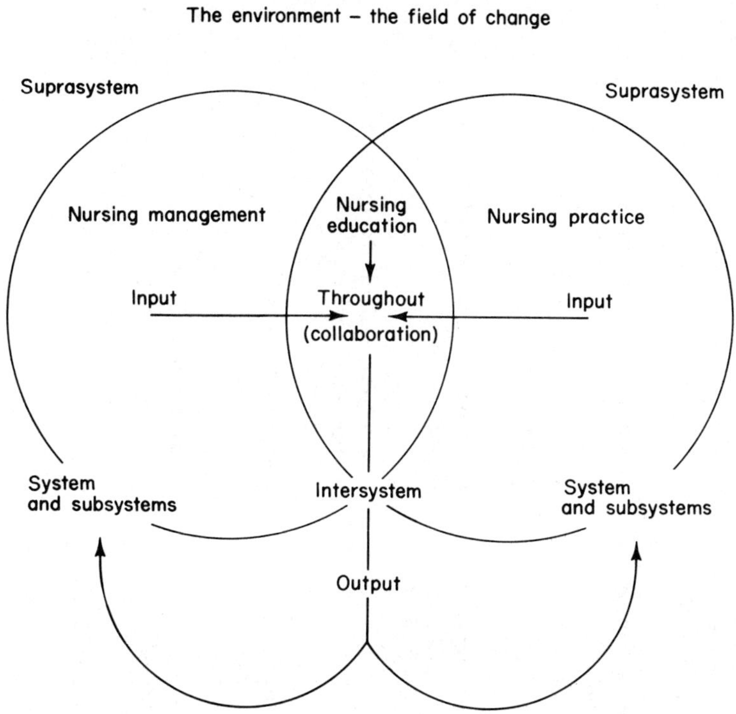

Fig. 7.5 A model for collaboration in change (from Archer, Kelly, and Bisch, 1984).

another, but that change arises from within and among the participants – i.e. the ward teams.

Recalling the key points of change in Chapter 2, at least one apparent invariable aspect of modern times is the tendency to change – and perhaps this aspect has always been an invariant? Here the educational aspect of change is widened, but continues to be contained in the same process of movement, growth, and development. Bennis, Benne, and Chinn (1985) see two pathways to change. One they call the 'law of non-intervention', the 'invisible hand' ideology of the *laissez-faire* doctrine. The other pathway to change is the 'law and radical intervention', represented at the opposite extreme by Marxist analysis. Chinn and Benne (1985) identify three types of strategy which illustrate these pathways to change (Fig. 7.6). The first group in this illustration is the

Table 7.1 Strategies of deliberate changing (from Chinn and Benne, 1985, pp. 44–5)

Rational/empirical	*Normative/re-educative*	*Power/coercive*
(Views of the Enlightenment and classical liberalism)	(Views of therapists, trainers, and situation changers)	(Use of political institutions)
Basic research and dissemination of knowledge through general education	Improving the problem-solving capabilities of a system	Strategies of non-violence (e.g. strikes, negotiations)
Personnel selection and replacement	Releasing and fostering growth in the persons who make up the system to be changed	Use of political institutions (e.g. ballot laws, judicial decisions)
Systems analysts as staff consultants		Changing through the recomposition and manipulation of power élites
Applied research and linkage systems for diffusion of research results	Freud (psychotherapy)	(Non-violent strategies) Gandhi
Utopian thinking as a strategy of changing	Rogers (counselling)	Martin Luther King
Perceptual and conceptual reorganization through the clarification of language	Lewin (research, training, action)	(Changing power élites) Marx

empirical/rational group of strategies, which assumes that people are rational and that they will follow their rational self-interest, once it is revealed to them. The second type of change strategy is known as normative/re-educative, where humans are seen to interact with their environment. Effective innovation requires a change of attitudes, relationships, values, and skills; therefore, the activity within and among people involves change agents – people such as ourselves. The use of power is instrumental in all three strategies of change. In the rational/empirical, knowledge is the major ingredient of power; the normative/re-educative strategies 'recognize the importance of noncognitive determinants of behaviour as resistances or supports to changing – values, attitudes, and feelings at the personal level and norms and relationships at the social level' (Chinn and Benne, 1985); the power/coercive strategies emphasize political and economic sanctions in the exercise of power.

The Management of Change Project attempted to use an approach of not intrusively intervening in the work of nurses by using strategies from all three aspects illustrated in Table 7.1 (The process of events which describe how this was done is described later in this chapter.) (See also discussion of Table 2.3 on p. 33.)

7.2 ACTIONING CHANGE THROUGH RESEARCH

Cultural and environmental influences upon people in mental hospitals became clear in the picture which emerged in Chapter 1, and the answer to any question about the way ahead must respect people's interaction with their social situation. The Management of Change Project has studied the social situation with a view to improving the quality of action within it (Chapter 3). The term 'action research' was coined by the social psychologist Kurt Lewin. He fled Nazi Germany and settled in the USA, where he discerned yet another degree of anti-Semitism and racism. Lewin stresses the need for cultural change as part of what the calls a 're-education process'. His model as a research and evaluative base for our study has proved itself congruent with the change theory which we used; it is consistent, too, with the problems in changing which are described in Chapter 2. This approach (and we have used this model to approach the study, not as a cut-and-dried formula) involves certain principles which have been outlined by Benne (1985), as follows:

1. Processes by which we acquire normal and abnormal behaviour are similar. There are common themes running through education and rehabilitation, for example, whether one is a nurse or a client. Regardless of who we are, or what our behaviour is like, all forward movement involves changes in thinking, feeling, and doing. So it is with backwards movement, whether this is, for example, professional misconduct or a challenging behaviour which is socially unacceptable;
2. Re-education must, as part of its process, make a cultural change. Consider the earlier example, in this chapter, of a management directive to implement a new nursing process format for documenting care. An attitude of acceptance, communications skill and self-awareness required to satisfy conditions implicit in the new format could make a run-down hospital ward a non-custodial, valuing culture. The nursing process cannot move forward unless these values are expressed by the people who are working, in their behaviour, never mind on paper. Re-education is about the change, or transformation of, for instance, one attitude to another. In the absence of re-education, counselling and therapy, now increasingly referred to by nurses, have traditionally sought to make changes with the individual, while paying little, if any, attention to the therapeutic setting. We have not in the past used change theory to inform our work;
3. Even extensive first-hand experience does not automatically create new thinking; experimental enquiry and discovery must be part of the educational and change process. Human growth and development characterize educational learning and distinguish it from non-educational learning (Chapter 2);
4. Social action, no less than physical action, is steered by perception. In Chapter 6 we have emphasized opening up the lines of communication; and Table 7.2 lists examples of structural changes which facilitate social and physical action. Even in the use of a research method, the accent is upon openness to new knowledge and new values *preceding* anticipated changes in perception and attitude. Habitual perceptions are challenged by

Table 7.2 Examples of structural changes in the management of change

1983	Teacher–senior nurse partnership for in-service training
1983	Methods of critical enquiry, e.g. observations, questionnaires, built-in to the nursing assistant training course
1983	School-based NA training devolves to mostly ward-based training, with sisters sharing teaching
1983	NA training includes ward-based teaching for whole ward teams, i.e. resuscitation procedure/skills, reality orientation
1983	NA Monitoring Group links with Nurse Practice Group, Hospital Procedure Committee, and Standards Working Party
1984	Feedback briefings for all levels/grades of staff to report results of 1983 NA evaluation, e.g. observations, etc.
1984	NA training curtailed and Monitoring Group disbanded, to establish a Management of Change Project Steering Group which aims to focus upon arrangement of educational needs for all nurses. Members of the Steering Group include senior tutor, assistant director of nursing services, and head of staff development department
1984	Five elderly care wards selected as sample for action research study
1984	Sister established as role model, as project impetus swings from focus upon NA to sisters' development programme
1985	Attempt to make permanent a ward establishment of nurses in the project area of five wards
1985	Appoint Evaluation Subgroup (of the Project Steering Group) to select measurement tools, e.g. Qualpacs, Monitor, something suited to the local project and devised by ourselves, and to implement findings from using the tool
1985	Re-introduction of nursing process, based upon new forms
1985	February–July weekly ward team groups, facilitated by teacher and senior nurse
1986	Teacher-facilitated once-a-fortnight Sisters' Groups
1986	Sisters' hours of duty change from shiftwork to 9 a.m.–5 p.m. each Thursday, accessing them for Sisters' Group, Quality Circles, and collaboration with one another around issues of restoring accountability, authority, and autonomy to ward management
1986	Introduction of ward team Quality Circles, once a fortnight
1986	Teambuilding/Assertion/Quality Nursing workshops for sisters/senior nurses
1986	Selection and use of Therapeutic Nursing Function Indicator for ward sisters

open exchange of feedback between members of the ward team groups;

5. As a rule, the possession of correct knowledge, say, to execute a nursing procedure such as filling in a lost-property form, does not compensate for or rectify false perceptions. Social perception is linked to self-perception, so that a nurse may *do* what is socially acceptable rather than what he/she thinks and/or feels is right;
6. Incorrect stereotypes (prejudices) are functionally equivalent to wrong concepts (theories). Benne (1985) relates the story of the man who believed he was dead. This man agreed that dead men don't bleed. When he agreed to have his finger pricked, he changed his mind and claimed that dead men do bleed. The point is that experience, *per se*, is inadequate to change a person's or group's theories of the world;
7. Changes in sentiments do not necessarily follow changes in cognitive structures. This principle of Lewin's stresses the relative independence between processes of cognitive change, of thinking, and changes in values, or sentiment. However, our argument in Chapter 2 is that thinking, feeling, and doing are related and the educational input of people such as ourselves is the link by which one area is transferred to another, i.e. thinking to feeling, to doing, and vice versa;
8. Further to point 2 in this series of principles about change, there are three ways of looking at the overall process. Like (a) re-education from point 2, (b) re-socialization and (c) re-enculturation are transformations from one state of being to another. Take for instance the so-called 'hidden curriculum' in nurse training. Students may learn more from what they do on ward placements than from what is taught in the school classroom. In a negative way, this can lead to students' adopting task-oriented approaches to care, if no continuing education opportunities are taken up by trained staff. An example of enculturation would be the use of nursing process (Fig. 7.1) and change-agents as culture-carriers, as a vehicle to establish values such as client-centred care. Values introduced in this way can transform a custodial culture to one where multidisciplinary working, for example, can have a chance to develop, once the values are assimilated and internalized by staff. These three different ways of looking at the change

process involve (a) a change in the way people pursue goals, a change in action-ideology, (b) a real acceptance of a changed set of facts and values and (c) a change in the way people see the social world;

9. Acceptance of a new set of values and beliefs cannot usually be brought about item by item. Therefore, a helping process towards change must include clarifying values for individual participants, that is, enabling people to maintain their identity and choice;
10. An individual accepts new values and beliefs by accepting his/her belonging within a group. Group meetings (Table 7.2) are an example of how new cultural values, for example, can be carried into a group and taken up to the benefit of individuals;

Action research, using change theory, is a link between self-evaluation and professional development. Change occurs in three steps, which Lewin calls 'unfreezing', 'moving toward a new level', and 'refreezing'. Unfreezing refers to the movement from a steady state to one that is unstable and amenable to change. It involves disturbing the equilibrium, or breaking the habit. The process described in Chapter 6 demonstrates how disequilibrium can help motivate people to collaborate in the change process, to use their active participation for self-assessment and forward movement personally, and to recognize the usefulness of this method in the process method of nursing. If the collaboration is successful, a higher level of behaviour is attained. Refreezing is the integration of this new learning with behaviour. The structural changes (Table 7.2) are supports which enable a higher level of thinking, feeling, and doing to be sustained until internalized.

7.3 CHANGING STRUCTURE

The situational analysis in Chapter 2 has identified a number of changes in the world of nursing at several different levels of the hierarchy; Fig. 7.7 is a reminder of some of the ideological shifts in nursing, which bring with them major change in the way we approach and go about our work. The Management of Change Project is (more or less) a microcosm of a larger whole.

The eighteen examples of structural change between 1983 and

Status ▶

Vocation		Profession
Patient	Nature of the recipient of care	Individual
Care	Nursing role	Care
Classical	Education	Romantic
Objectives	Curriculum model	Process
Subjects	Content	Themes
Convergent	Learning style	Divergent
Didactic Instruction	Methodology	Discovery
In Authority Ritual	Teacher–student relationship	An authority/ co-operation
Tests (Teacher Set)	Assessment	Personal growth and development
Psychometric	Nursing research	Ethnographic

Fig. 7.7 Overview from the literature, reflecting shifting ideologies in nursing and nursing education.

1986 (Table 7.2) demonstrate a significant shift in focus. In 1983 the attention was upon the nursing assistant training, and in 1986 ward sisters were at the centre of the study. People unfamiliar with the project have said, about this shift in focus, 'Well, why aren't you paying attention to nursing assistants any more?' We found from the nursing assistant course that for nursing assistants to progress in their work, changes had to be made in both educational and managerial support for ward sisters, which was lacking.

While there is a great deal of evidence to indicate that we operated within the area of Lewin's ten principles of re-education, we altered our direction as a result of data coming from the changes which are exampled in Table 7.2. A strict adherence to Lewin's model might not allow such a shift to take place. Also we performed much analysis with the people involved in the study before trying to use the feedback to implement new ideas. For example, in 1983 the nursing assistant training course became a formal monitoring system. Feedback from the nursing assistants' questionnaires and teachers' observations, and the interviews with nursing assistants, resulted in four structural changes during 1983 (Table 7.2). When the information coming back from the nursing assistants was eventually shared with all grades of staff, including senior nurses, the picture began to emerge that no amount of training, as such, would be adequate to increase the quality of care. What was required became open to question. By introducing the prospect of critical enquiry as a formal part of groups, e.g. in the nursing assistants' training course, it became possible for people never before consulted as equal participants in care to be vocal and instrumental in sharing the responsibility for change.

The first change was making formal through the senior tutor and director of nursing services a partnership between the in-service teacher and an experienced senior nurse. This pair reported to a Monitoring Group. The mix of thinking, feeling, and doing which they designed in the nursing assistants' course became the foundation upon which the project was built. Action research provided an evaluative element, but most important, it added the 'spiral of cycles' generated by participants on the course and subsequently their 'qualified' colleagues upon the wards of the hospital.

The teacher as researcher and practitioner, the teacher–senior nurse partnership, and the valued voice from the shop floor, as it were are changes that altered the structure of the way nurses work. These changes have implications for cultural values in the hospital because, for example, a process method is immediately being fostered by the way in which questions arise and the very nature of questions. For the nursing assistants, and clients' visitors for that matter, the question was not in what way is it right to do a thing, but the pertinent question involves what people are doing and how they can be enhanced in achieving what they set out to do. There are a number of examples in Chapter 6 of the difficulties with attitudes and perceptions which would require more than a thinking and behavioural approach to nurses' and clients' needs.

During 1984, following regular feedback briefings which were to become a hallmark of the Management of Change Project, dramatic changes came as a result of the findings during 1983 (Table 7.2). The Nursing Assistant Monitoring Group became the Project Steering Group as training was discontinued. In place of training for nursing assistants, the study sought to examine how all nurses could benefit educationally and how standards of care could be raised. Although this chapter has been about the structural changes that were introduced, we should point out that regular meetings of a new group, whether the ward team meetings facilitated by a senior nurse and a teacher or the collaborative Steering Group meetings, or the facilitators support group, Sisters' Group, or Quality Circles on all five project wards, would all be dead without the processes that occurred within and around them. However, the task of this chapter has been to illustrate the nature of structural changes and how they can facilitate process and outcome change by, for example, structuring collaborative participation, i.e. people working alongside one another towards a common goal of furthering their understanding and their skills in enchanced client care.

One of the structural changes which never really worked was the attempt to make a permanent establishment on the five project wards. This change struck at the heart of the nursing officers' management strategy. The hospital had always been manned on the basis of pulling a nurse from here and slotting her there, despite sister's view, for example, or the nurses' plans for the clients. Some of the nursing officers simply refused to honour the director of nursing services instructions, in the same way in which the nursing assistants would refuse to honour sisters' instructions. Nursing assistants, or junior qualified nurses, could, for instance, go directly 'over the head' of sister to make arrangements with nursing officers, as they were then called. The Hospital Advisory Service (1986) found no examples of good practice under these conditions. However, there were enough nursing officers/senior nurses who believed in and supported the project to enable other structural changes actually to work; for example, during the 1985 weekly ward team group meetings, senior nurses attended the groups with a teacher-facilitator to share the nurses' concerns (Chapter 6). The Sisters' Groups and the change in their duty rota to allow them to work alongside each other for six months, at the direction of the nursing manager, was ignored openly by only one senior nurse. The disciplinary procedure in the hospital seemed on the one hand to create apprehension of the time taken by professional bodies if there was trouble. On the other hand there was anxiety about the manning-the-hospital difficulties which could result from a dispute. The products, or outcomes, of the structural changes (Table

7.2) are the subject of the chapters about process methods, but here suffice it to say that the eighteen examples of structural change presented in Table 7.2 represent some of the new ways of working together which valued and used contributions of the shopfloor nurses.

7.4 CONCLUSION

The role of the project Steering Group was to propose and support change which resulted from the evaluations which continually took place on the five elderly care wards. This representative group from education, management, and practice in terms of the five participating wards sought to change certain working arrangements to foster a process method of nursing and to make structural changes which opened the lines of communication between people upon the wards. Because of the custodial attitudes and task-centred focus of the original nursing, the educational emphasis was geared to fostering attitudes and perceptual change through participation in the project. The daily ward handover at 1.30–2.30 p.m., for example, became a venue for internalizing changes. These changes arose from the apparent routine and ritual of the daily tasks of ward nursing. When all members of the team were encouraged to participate in the ward team meetings, it became clear that the nurses were wanting changes and, in particular, a change to firm leadership from sister. There was a structure in the routine patterns of nursing which was upset by the project, and these new structures of open communication were the receptacle of anxiety in their early months (Chapter 4).

The implications of using change theory have been evident from the start of the Management of Change Project. Personal resistance is a major but separate issue and is therefore discussed in Chapter 4. The nursing process was introduced during the period 1983–6 when the project was influencing innovation on several fronts, especially in other groups concerned about falling standards of care. Innovation within a hospital, but only within a small part of the hospital, has clear disadvantages. This was evident in the difficulty which senior nurses had in supporting the project. One example of this difficulty among senior nurses was absenteeism in Ward Team Staff Support Groups. Another difficulty for these managers was letting-go of the power they inherited, from the custodial hospital culture of the past. Senior nurses' task-oriented interventions in practicalities of ward life had interfered with sisters' chances to develop as team leaders. However, the initiative of the Management of Change Project owed its livelihood to the support of most of the senior nurses. The age-old customs of running a workhouse-cum asylum-cum-hospital made it difficult to translate any concern for the process and individuality of care into reality. It may, in our experience, be too much to expect to ever have unconditional permission for change of any kind. The implication from our work is that careful collaboration and analysis of a suitable evaluation method can perhaps only prepare nurses and clients for a range of options. There is a risk of leaving staff and clients behind if, in pursuit of change, projects are aimed only at advancing professional interests and not client interests. As long as staff are in a place where to work is to work like others have in the past and to be with clients is to be like managers have been with staff in the past, then person-centred care is impossible. Actioning, structuring and evaluating change has been about developing ways of critical discovery, to enable staff to liberate themselves and their clients. Until staff are valued as individuals, clients and staff will suffer from the humanizing effects of former psychiatric hospital regimes. The profession of nursing with its systems theory, code of conduct, and practitioners' accountability, has put itself in a top–down position (Chapter 1). The Management of Change Project worked from the bottom up which means at times from the chaos which the nurses experience within themselves and in the ward environment. We found in the various structural changes it experienced that firm top-down leadership in nursing had to co-exist with respect for bottom-up values. While the Sisters' Groups and Quality Circles showed that such co-existence was possible, too many conflicting variables impinged upon nursing leadership, which was still influenced by the heritage of conflicts (Chapter 1).

However, the structures of the project were used to establish model training wards for the statutory registered mental nurse training, and within the year there was an explosion of management changes, including the replacement of the senior nurses of the hospital by patient services managers and the first concrete closure strategy under the leadership of a new unit general manager.

It is not in the spirit of our work to generalize any apparent results to other hospitals or to the nursing profession itself. However, the evidence from the process chapters in this book suggests that these new structures were instrumental in change, particularly in fostering attitudes positively affecting client-centred care and respect for the values of others, both colleagues and non-nurses.

The way in which change occurs for each individual is threefold: by changes in cognition, or thinking; by changes in affect, or feeling; and by changes in conation, or doing. For these internal changes to achieve an interface with a receptive-to-change environment and become internal structural changes, we had created new structures (Table 7.2) to facilitate change. The desired effect was to foster perceptions and attitudes conducive to a process method of individualized nursing care. The entire Management of Change Project was influenced by its own early findings during the NA training course. The structures devised to implement changes were, for example, the Sisters' Group, and the ward team meetings facilitated by a teacher and senior nurse. We are involved in a process of supporting people during the restructuring of their experience. It is not just a change from doing something one way to doing it another way. What is most important about change is people's changing experience. One of the most difficult problems is coping with the uncertainty of whether doing something different will work. For example, there is a risk in moving away from task-oriented care, as is indicated for instance by patients' bathing and bowel-movement checklists, to a focus on clarifying with a client their lifestyle preferences, ranging from personal care to social events. Learning opportunities in the transition to new experience is the subject of Chapter 2. Where the ward nurses were satisfied with existing routine, it is interesting to note that the changing structure was used to iron out wide ranging differences in how each other's roles were perceived, as was evident in Chapter 6. Thus while changing of structures is inextricably tied to the process of the project, the new structures themselves were radical changes which evolved logically from the rationale of the early findings in the NA training course.

Changing structure, for example, introducing a new format for the nursing process, was designed to increase participation, to empower nurses to use their personal and professional authority, and to facilitate nursing accountability. The new structures were also the containers for individuals' educational development. The teaching, in this sense, took place within the new structures and was part and parcel of the ongoing Management of Change Project. Given the situational analysis described in Chapter 2, it would not have been possible to try out new methods without the new structures to support them.

REFERENCES

Altschul, A.T. (1983) 'The consumer's voice: nursing implications'. *Journal of Advanced Nursing*, **8**, 175–183.

Archer, S.E., Kelly, C.D., and Bisch, S.A. (1984) *Implementing Change in Communities: A Collaborative Process*, C.V. Mosby, St Louis, Mo.

Beck, C.M., Rawlins, R.P. and Williams, S.R. (eds) (1984), *Mental Health – Psychiatric Nursing: A Holistic Life-cycle Approach*, C.V. Mosby, St Louis, Mo.

Bennis, K.D. (1985) the processes of re-education: an assessment of Kurt Lewin's views, in W.G. Bennis, K.D. Benne, and R. Chinn (eds) *The Planning of Change*, 4th edn, Holt, Rinehart and Winston, New York.

Bennis, W.G., Benne, K.D. and Chinn, R. (eds) (1985) *The Planning of Change*, 4th edn, Holt, Rinehart and Winston, New York.

Bergman, R. (1986) Nursing in a changing world. *International Nursing Review*, **33**(4), 110–16.

Bloch, D. (1975) Evaluation of nursing care in terms of process and outcome – issues in research and quality assurance. *Nursing Research,* **24**(4), July–August, 256–63.

Chinn, R. and Benne, K.D. (1985) General strategies for effecting changes in human systems, in W.G. Bennis, K.D. Benne and R. Chinn (eds) *The Planning of Change*, 4th edn, Holt, Rinehart and Winston, New York, pp. 22–45.

Clark, J. (1983) Problems of evaluation in preventive health-care, in J. Clark and J. Henderson (eds) *Community Health*, London, pp. 265, 268, 270–1.

Cormack, D.F.S. (1984) *The Research Process in Nursing*, Blackwell Scientific, Oxford.

Donabedian, A. (1966) Evaluating the quality of medical care. *Milbank Memorial Fund Quarterly*, July, **44**, pt 2, 166–206.

Donabedian, A. (1969) Some issues in evaluating the quality of nursing care. *Am. J. Public Health*, **59**, 1833–6.

Fox, R.N. and Venture, M.R. (1984) Internal psychometric characteristics of the Quality Patient Care Scale, *Nursing Research*, **33**(2), March–April, pp. 112–17.

George, J.B. (Chairman) (1985) *Nursing Theories: The Base for Professional Nursing Practice*, Prentice-Hall Inc., Englewood Cliffs, N.J.

Given, B., Given, C.W. and Simoni, L.E. (1979) Relationships of processes of care to patient outcomes. *Nursing Research,* **28**(2), March–April, 85–93.

Henderson, V. (1969) *The Nature of Nursing*, Macmillan, New York.

Hospital Advisory Service (1986) *The Report of a Visit to Tooting Bec Hospital, South London*, HAS, Beckenham, Kent.

Hughes, F. (1985) What do nurses do? *Senior Nurse*, **2**(4), January, 18–19.

Lathlean, J. (1983) The Ward Sister Training Project. *The Evaluation of an Experimental Training Scheme for Ward Sisters,* Chelsea College, University of London.

Luker, K.A. (1984) An overview of evaluation research in nursing. *Journal of Advanced Nursing*, **6**, 81–93.

McFarlane, E.A. (1980) Nursing theory: comparison of four theoretical proposals. *Journal of Advanced Nursing*, **5**, 3–19.

McFarlane, J.K. and Castledine, G. (1982) *A Guide to the Practice of Nursing using the Nursing Process*, C.V. Mosby, St Louis, Mo.

McGovern, W.N. and Rodgers, J.A. (1986) Change theory. *American Journal of Nursing*, May, 566–7.

Nodder, T. (Chairman) (1980) *Organisation and Management Problems of Mental Illness Hospitals*, HMSO, London.

Price, B. and Sculthorpe (1985) Should nurses diagnose? *Senior Nurse,* **2**(4), January, 8–12.

Quinn, S.M. (Chairperson) (1981) *Towards Standards: A Discussion Document. Second Report of the RCN Working Committee on Standards of Nursing Care (England and Wales)*, Royal College of Nursing, London.

Roper, N., Logan, N.W. and Tierney, A. (1981). *Learning to Use the Process of Nursing*, Churchill Livingstone, London.

Ryan, B.J. (1979) Nursing care plans: a systems approach to developing criteria for planning and evaluation, in A. Marriner (ed.) *The Nursing Process: A Scientific Approach to Nursing Care*, 2nd edn, C.V. Mosby, St Louis, Mo, pp. 249–58.

Stanton, M., Paul, C. and Reeves, J.S. (1985) An overview of the Nursing Process, in J.B. George (ed.) *Nursing Theories: The Base for Professional Nursing Practice*, 2nd edn, Prentice-Hall, Englewood Cliffs, NJ, pp. 14–33.

Stuart, G.W. and Sundeen, S.J. (eds) (1983) *Principles and Practice of Psychiatric Nursing,* 2nd edn, C.V. Mosby, St Louis, Mo.

Urdang, L. and Swallow, H.H. (eds) (1983) *Mosby's Medical and Nursing Dictionary*. C.V. Mosby, St Louis, Mo.

Ward, M.F. (1985) *The Nursing Process in Psychiatry*, Churchill Livingstone, London.

Wattley, L.A. and Muller, D.J. (1984) *Investigating Psychology: A Practical Approach for Nursing*, Harper and Row, London.

World Health Organisation (1979) *Nursing Services: Report on a WHO Symposium in Stuttgart, 1978,* WHO, Copenhagen.

Wright, D. (1984) An introduction to the evaluation of nursing care: a review of the literature. *Journal of Advanced Nursing,* **9**, 457–67.

— 8 —
Outstanding issues

8.1 INTRODUCTION

It is the nature of life that often what you originally conceived of was a straightforward matter, in reality, proves to be far more complex. In our work with facilitating change, we have not been surprised to find that the process of change is indeed complex. Rather what has surprised us is that the specific work we were involved in has thrown up so many issues and questions.

Like all good researchers we have tried, in our discussions about the work, to return to the original questions and aims of that work. We accepted that in using an action research framework there would be subtle changes to our original intentions but the Steering Group meetings, the ward team meetings, the Quality Circles, and all the other comings together, raised so many issues that we, in our naïvety, had not foreseen. These issues ranged from 'What do we do when the hospital closes?' to 'What shall we wear coming to work?'

This chapter seeks to examine these issues in the context of facilitating change in general terms. We have taken a selection of the many issues raised and present them here to illustrate how interesting working with change can be. Some of the issues might be perceived as problematic or difficult, but we tend to view them as the exciting and challenging products of working with change. We have benefited from dealing with these and other issues, and they have helped shape the model that we propose in the final chapter of the book. It is also interesting to observe that from an organizational point of view the airing of many of these issues has been enormously beneficial.

8.2 VALUES IN THE WORK

In the preceding chapters we have discussed various values that we, as teacher and researcher, held about our work. In any attempt to introduce change it is vitally important to know exactly what these values are and to keep them in the forefront of one's thinking. At the beginning of our work we did make a few assumptions, based on the work we had done and were doing as nurses.

Bottom up

It appeared to us that there were two diametrically opposed means to approaching the task of facilitating change. One was to introduce change by decree, from the top downwards. The latter part of our work was caught up in just such a change, following the recommendations of the Griffiths Report (1984). We had previously experienced several attempts to introduce change in such a manner that was less than successful. Within the hospital in which we worked, there had been one such attempt to introduce the 'nursing process'. A memo from top management had been issued with an identified start date and supporting documentation. The documentation was duly introduced on the appointed day (1st April 1985), but this was without any accompanying change in the approach to care or the way in which nurses habitually thought. Thus the evaluation sheets of the nursing process documents still read: 'slept well', 'satisfactory night', and 'all care given', as opposed to a detailed evaluation of each problem that was addressed during the shift.

The second approach, and the one that we have grown to value is the so-called 'bottom-up' method. In essence, this meant involving those people whom the changes concerned; and at the beginning of our work, we had the intuitive sense that this was indeed the way to move forward. After all, nursing is about involving, and being involved with, people; and much of what we do as nurses is concerned with helping people 'work it through', whether it is a temporary physical ailment or a confused and unclear mind, or coming to terms with death. It is interesting to reflect that the work with nurses concerning change is very similar to the work nurses themselves do with their patients-clients. Again and again, in both areas, the ideas of involving people and working it through come up.

Where people are

Moving on to the second assumption/value that we made about the work was a logical extension of working with people from the bottom up, that is beginning the process of change from where people are, in terms of attitude, understanding, knowledge, or any other state. As we have explained in previous chapters, we spent much time checking out and trying to understand the situation into which we were going, and the people we were to work alongside. Later in this chapter we shall briefly outline the rules, mostly unwritten, that govern all settings and especially the institutional setting. It is our belief that it is impossible to achieve any concrete change without first making some attempt to understand the situation. Utilizing the knowledge gained about the people and their situation, one knows how, and at what level, to pitch any intervention. Moreover, it is possible to judge the speed at which to proceed most effectively. Without this knowledge, there is a great risk not of just failing to secure change, but also a danger of alienating those targeted for change. The introduction of the 'nursing process', described earlier, is a good example of where no attempt was made to start introducing the change from where the nursing and the nurses were on the wards, the consequence being that they just continued doing what they had always done and that attitudes became further entrenched.

Research

From the previous chapters, it is clear that the third value we held about the work was that evaluation was of great usefulness, and it became an essential part of our armoury both in the way that it involved people and could be used by them: thus our choice was action research, as we have already described. At the beginning of the work, and at many points as it progressed, there were clamours for us to show that change was occurring. As a team facilitating change in nursing, we were concerned with how the research could help us in the process of change. What information could it provide, what did it tell us about the dynamics of the situation? In any change situation, both elements are important. Unfortunately, we often neglect the informative nature of research in favour of the satisfaction over the fact that change, often of a physical nature, has occurred. There is a tendency to view the closure of long-stay psychiatric beds as being a successful change without consideration of how it has affected the people involved.

Standards

In seeking to introduce change, most people have a fairly clear idea of where the change is taking them; and certainly, they have a clear idea of the component parts. In our work, we were not exceptional. We had a clear idea in our minds of how we saw nursing, and these values have been expanded in Chapter 1. In the project, we were seeking to move people along the path that led to these values. We tried not to pitch our expectations too high.

We challenged and wanted people on the wards to think about their nursing. Where was the thought process we call the 'nursing process' going, what was it offering to the people it involved, and how was it best organized? We also had a clear idea as to how our aim was to be achieved. Our standard was that we encouraged people to be involved, not just the sister but the whole of the team; and we wanted patients to be involved and people from elsewhere in the hospital.

One fascinating product of the work was that we put together all our discussion about standards and produced a Patients' Bill of Rights; this is reproduced in the appendix. Although we did not in fact use this as a basis for more work on the setting and monitoring standards, it nevertheless represents the standards implicit in our work. Similar statements have been used in our later work in other settings.

8.3 ETHICS

Many books (e.g. Benjamin and Curtis 1986; Tschudin, 1986; Faulder, 1985) and papers (e.g. Melia, 1987; Warnock, 1985; Stephenson and Moran, 1987) have been written on the ethics of both research and nursing. In any research work, a thorough examination of the ethical implications is vital. We had few worries about the way in which we were approaching the work. Our values were those that the literature told us were important. We have already discussed the changes taking place in mental health services, and our work was to do with part of these changes and preparing people for them. We intended to do nothing invasive and were not involving patients or carers directly.

However, we draw attention to the broad subject of 'ethics', first, because we were frequently asked 'Whose permission do you have to do this work?', and second, because we were continually aware of the pressure, perceived by the people we worked with, to participate in the work.

In nursing as we suspect in other professions, there is a great suspicion and apprehension of research. Perhaps because investigation or observation by 'outsiders' has frequently been associated with discipline, research is often viewed negatively. Unless this barrier is overcome, then the work is hampered. We have talked elsewhere about the ways we overcame barriers, talking to people, being honest and fair, listening and being there and involved.

Initially there was some evidence of protest about being involved in research. It took the form of disruptive behaviour in groups (arriving late or wandering off in the middle). Many of our initial interventions were seen as threatening, suggesting that the nurses were uncaring or unsafe. A lot of time was spent in open and frank discussions in the groups. This helped allay the anxieties but it was a process that required much time and effort. Returning to the wards a year or so after the end of the work, a frequent comment is 'We never really realized the value of your work with us until you left'; and unfortunately, that is an altogether too common finding in the business of health care.

Thus we dealt with the suspicions and apprehensions, but it is probably true to say that we never overcame them entirely. The culture of the institution meant that we were asked many times 'What are you doing', 'Who are you doing it for?', and 'Who gave you permission?'. The answer to the last question was: 'You gave us permission', a concept that was often difficult for people to accept!

Participation in the project was, of course, voluntary. Faced with seemingly high-powered representatives from management, education, and research, it was difficult for a sister, let alone members of her team, to decline. One ward did drop out of the original project group for a variety of reasons, and we respected anyone's decision not to participate. As the work developed, the perceived pressure to take part grew less. Conversely, there grew a pressure from within many of the groups for the ward to continue to be part of the project.

In working with change, we think it is important to be aware that people grasp ideas and understanding at different times. For those not as quick or not as committed as others, there are pressures from both the team and from individuals within it. Therefore, the pace of change needs to be carefully controlled to enable the majority to ride with it. A listening ear needs to be kept open for those who are finding the pace too great.

8.4 RULES

In Turner's (1974) book on ethnomethodology various authors, including Goffman, talk about how there are unwritten rules governing any gathering or collection of people. In institutions it appears that there are two sets of rules. One set contains the policies and procedures that are written down, and the other contains those rules held by the people within the institution but not written down. In Turner's book there is reference to the rules operating in prisons, for instance.

Undoubtedly it is true that there were two such sets of rules in the setting in which we were working. If you refer back to Table 6.1 on the normal daily ward routine (p. 116), you can see an example of the second set of rules. This typical routine was not written down anywhere, nor handed down from the managers. It was just the agreed way in which the ward ran. It was simple, easy, and comfortable for the staff to operate. Any attempt to change the rules met with fierce resistance and could lead to an individual being ostracized in the team. Any attempts by outsiders to change the routine were fought off and the team closed ranks.

The reason we draw attention to the unspoken rules is that they are extremely important to the people working within them. Changing the rules is very difficult to do, except through the group as a whole, and that takes a lot of work. Charging into areas where you are ignorant of the rules causes many problems. So it is well worth taking time to discover how a group of people operate, what are the rules that govern their work. It is going back to the values that we espoused earlier in starting where people are.

Take one everyday example. In conversation you hardly ever have two people speaking at once and the conversational handover is very finely co-ordinated (down to microseconds). Clearly, there are a set of rules operating that allow us to achieve these outcomes. When people break these rules, there are difficulties and often disdain for the person breaking the rule, e.g. interrupting. Thus being aware of and attempting to understand the rules of the situation into which you are seeking to introduce change is of vital importance.

8.5 OWNERSHIP

One of the keys to the success of our work in facilitating change has been the fact that the people involved have become an integral part of the whole project. As we have shown, we were particularly careful to get people involved, and that our use of an action research framework has been beneficial. The fact that people could read about their team and its work helped them to feel in control and a part of what was going on. The facilitators were careful, in all the groups, that the individual's and the group's efforts were valued, by being highlighted, discussed, and praised – both in the group and in other forums. For instance, this meant praising seemingly small and insignificant occurrences such as a new and colourful poster.

All these factors helped people feel that it was their project, and it engendered pride in what they had achieved. One occurrence that brought this home was after we had presented the work at a conference, when we were greeted on our return by several people saying that they should have been involved and given the opportunity to talk about 'their' work. Others wanted their part in the work mentioned not, we perceived, in a fit of pique, but because they felt genuinely part of it.

8.6 CULTURE OF THE ENVIRONMENT

For those who have worked in large psychiatric hospitals, much of the detail we have used as examples must be familiar. Nursing the mentally ill in large institutions has its place in the history of psychiatric nursing, as we have outlined in Chapter 1. Whatever one's views about such institutions, there is no doubting the profound influence of them on the people involved, both patients and staff. Wherever an attempt is made to introduce change, there is a whole culture to take into account, particularly if that culture has developed and matured. Any change must take this into account.

In the setting in which we were working with change, a whole range of factors created and nurtured the culture. Nurses followed a traditional care progression that involved conforming to the organizational philosophy and doing a fair share of the work. Eventually you were rewarded by promotion. In an environment rock solid in its Victorian brick buildings, semi-isolated from the community around it, things changed very little. Bits of the furniture were decades old, kitchens on the wards had actually become 'trendy' because of their antiquity. Old iron pipes pumped out uncontrollable heat or none at all. Some changes were so slow that they were unremarkable: other changes, though minor in nature, were greeted as major upheavals. This environment moulded people and easily absorbed any non-conformers. The routines reflected the permanence of the buildings. No one really thought about the effectiveness of their work because the culture told them everything was running smoothly. Even critical visits by outside agencies were put to one side when related to the culture. Things worked well, people were happy, and outsiders just did not understand.

There was a social fabric to this institution: groupings of people from certain ethnic groups were strong and tended to be self-perpetuating. People knew each other and each other's business, any potential for disturbance being regulated within these groups. There was a strong pressure for people to get on with the job and not to 'rock the boat'. Over the years one of the ways in which this pressure manifested itself was the constraints on budgets. This led to a change in the skill mix of nursing staff on the wards with a gradual increase in the number of untrained staff. Any protest from the sisters on the wards was quietly smoothed over, using the social networks that were so well established.

The importance of the culture needs to be understood by anyone contemplating change within it. As with the rules, an attempt needs to be made to uncover what is going on, and to try to understand it. Attempting change straight away usually results in the defences going up in a most organized way! The way past the culture appears to involve bypassing the key owners of it and importing outsiders, as has been tried in several institutions. However, that is a fairly drastic solution; getting into the culture can be very beneficial, acceptance within the community/culture putting the facilitator in a strong negotiating position.

8.7 DEVELOPING PEOPLE

Change affects people in many different ways. We have already examined the feelings of mistrust and suspicion that it can engender. In our work, we came across many other responses to our work with change.

'Tell us what we are to do.'
'I don't understand what you are saying.'
'I don't know.'
'Show us.'

In the group work, the facilitators worked hard to explain to people about the values in the work. They spent much time helping individuals and the group work through their uncertainties. Time was spent with people writing care plans and discussing problems. However, there was a limit to the resources of the project team. Issues, such as assertiveness training or communication skills training, could not be sufficiently dealt with in the groups.

If individuals are to cope with and come to terms with changes, then resources have to be made available to support them. It is no good half-way through a programme of change suddenly identifying needs and not being able to meet them. This strands people and leaves them feeling fairly negative. It is no good publishing an edict that the nursing process will be introduced without providing help for the people who are to use it. How will they understand what it is about and how to make use of it.

The way in which the management of change project was set up lent itself to being able to identify and meet the educational needs of people as they arose. The collaboration between education and management proved of great value. The educationists were secure in the knowledge that what they provided was actually what was required, as opposed to the traditional practice of providing broad, across-the-board generalist courses. The managers were happy because they were now able to identify that the education being provided met needs that would ultimately help them in managing.

8.8 CONTINUITY

It seems a little obvious to say that a project or programme is marked by a beginning and an end; however, we found it important to recognize this fact early on. Where a programme of change is introduced, there is always the danger that once the facilitator has left, the effects of change will be lost and people will return to their previous practices.

Without being melodramatic, there is also the real sense of loss that people feel when support ever present over a number of years is suddenly gone. There are parallels in the care of patients. Once you introduce greater continuity of care, you have to develop an individual's independence, so that they do not become too reliant on the key worker. A delicate balance is required to be maintained.

We encountered both problems, and we were required to address them early on. We sought out structural mechanisms by which people might continue the work and move on towards new values in the work. The structural support was most important. In any situation where a change agent withdraws his/her input, the nature of the change that occurs subsequently is different – at the least the pace of change slows, and at worst positive change ceases in favour of a return to a former position.

The success of the project in demonstrating that a particular kind of educational intervention facilitated change influenced the way in which the further education was to be conducted. The project had shown that conventional approaches to education in this setting, 'take-away' education, had little effect. In mental health great changes were occurring, e.g. the move towards community and the closure of traditional institutions, and these were reflected in the syllabus for trainee nurses. Therefore, educational managers were led into looking at how these changes might be supported.

8.9 MODEL WARD TRAINING

A specific result of the project was the establishment of a new approach to the business of education in the area of mental health; it provided continuity, as we described in the previous section. More important, it took on lessons that had been learnt. It established a group of wards that were to be used for educating nurses and provided for these wards by the following:

1. A facilitator to work with the nurses on the wards;
2. A philosophy that incorporated the values of:
   (a) groupwork
   (b) evaluation
   (c) action research
   (d) involving people
   (e) communicating
3. Specific objectives;
4. Management collaboration and support.

The success of the work is recorded elsewhere (Alstead, 1987), and we mention it to illustrate how working with change is productive.

8.10 INTERFERENCE

In our discussions about this book, we thought a lot about including a section with such a negative title as this. We decided to include it because, whenever people work for change, there are always others who feel unsure or threatened by that work. In an ideal world these uncertainties and fears are articulated and worked through. However, there are occasions, particularly in large organizations like the health service, when people do not express their views and, more important, try to thwart attempts to introduce change.

On the whole, we managed to bring issues within our work into the open. We were faced at times with attempts to limit or control the work. We suspect the reasons for this are complex, but intuitively we felt there were two factors: (a) the nature of change, exploring new ground, challenging the status quo, requiring people to let go a little; and (b) the power struggles that go on in organizations for control and ascendancy.

Perhaps we, as researchers, are most at risk? We had a vested interest in completing the work and collecting data that we could use and there was possibly a temptation to quicken the pace of change. This meant that we had to listen to and examine even more carefully the feedback that we got from the people with whom we were working.

In the collaborative situation in which we were working there were several examples of 'interference'. Within the hospital in which we undertook the project the most influential group of people were the senior nurse managers (the nursing officers). Their influence arose not because they were deciding on policy or participating in the planning of service, but rather because of their relationship with the majority care providers, the nurses. Edicts or orders came from on high about whatever, but these were the managers who were charged with implementing them. More important, feedback from the wards went through them, and they were at liberty to interpret it as they saw fit. The system worked very efficiently and most of these managers were extremely caring people. However, on occasions they could stifle initiative or at least make the introduction of change rather difficult. Here a prime example was the system employed by the senior nurse managers of 'booking out' (the movement of people for part/all of a shift from their regular place of work to cover for absent staff) nurses from the wards, which kept the organization moving forward but affected both the quality and continuity of care.

The willingness of several of these nursing officers to become involved in our collaborative study was a great credit to their courage. From a management point of view, it would have been far easier to ignore us. Involvement meant that their traditional methods of operation were challenged and that they had to take on board some new ideas.

Educationists also found the business of collaboration to be challenging. Conventional approaches and their sole control of teaching had to be re-thought in public. At times, strongly held views limited the development of the project and the onus of proof (showing that change was occurring) often interfered with the natural development of the work. A change agent, then, needs to be aware of the potential for negative pressures that can be exerted.

There is no need for paranoia, but an awareness of the problems does help and ways should be found to bring the issues into the open.

8.11 GENERAL MANAGEMENT

Within the health service the management changes following the Griffiths Report (1984) have had a profound effect on the organization of the service, although this is not the place to debate the relative merits or otherwise of those changes. However, within the new structures we think there is a place for the values we have aspired to: collaboration, groupwork, action research, and involving people. We note with considerable concern that some general managers do not share this view; they hold as paramount the accountability of the manager, and decision-making occurs in isolation.

Here we would only note what the report itself states about the success or otherwise of the management changes:

> the primary objective for health authorities in implementing the report's recommendations must be to achieve changes at unit level and below. If there were no observable improvements in services at that level, *in the eyes of patients and the community*, within 3–5 years, then there would have been no point in making changes at DHA level and above.
>
> (Griffiths Report, 1984, para. 6)

If indeed there are no changes, then perhaps we can commend to managers the methods in this book.

REFERENCES

Alstead, R. (1987) *Model Ward Project: Adult Mental Health, Tooting Bec Hospital, Phase 1*, August 1986–February 1987. Nightingale School of Nursing, London.

Benjamin, M. and Curtis, J. (1986) *Ethics in Nursing*, 2nd edn, Oxford University Press, Oxford.

Faulder, C. (1985) *Whose Body Is It*? Virago Press, London.

Griffiths, R. (Chairman) (1984) *NHS Management Inquiry* HMSO, London.

Melia, K. (1987) Everyday ethics for nurses: to lie or not to lie. *Nursing*

Times, **83**, 21 Jan., pp. 30–32.

Stephenson, M. and Moran, L. (1987) The dilemma of ethics *Senior Nurse*, **7**(3), Sept.

Tschudin, U. (1986) *Ethics in Nursing: the caring relationship*, Heinemann, London.

Warnock, M. (1985) Law and the pursuit of knowledge. *Conquest* (Research Defence Society), No. 175.

APPENDIX A: A PATIENTS' BILL OF RIGHTS

Second draft by the Steering Group for the Management of Change at Tooting Bec Hospital, West Lambeth Health Authority.

1. The right to appropriate treatment in a setting and under conditions most supportive of and least restrictive to personal liberty.
2. The right to know reasons for treatment, adverse affects, and available alternatives.
3. The right to an individualised, written nursing care plan, periodic review of care and evaluation of the plan.
4. The right to participate in care planning, having knowledge of nursing diagnosis and nursing action.
5. The right not to receive treatment except in an emergency or as permitted by law.
6. The right not to participate in experimentation.
7. The right to freedom from untherapeutic restraint or seclusion.
8. the right to a humane environment.
9. The right to confidentiality of records.
10. The right of access to telephone use, mail and visitors.
11. The right to know these rights.
12. The right to assert grievances when rights are infringed.
13. The right to referral when discharged.

— 9 —
A model for change

9.1 INTRODUCTION

In preparing this final chapter we have been struck by how important the practice of change has been to health care in general. The history of the National Health Service (NHS) is littered with attempts to force the natural pace of change, or to introduce radical change. We have made reference in previous chapters to the introduction of the 'nursing process', the Griffiths Report (1984), the closure of large psychiatric institutions, and many other large- and small-scale changes. You do not need to look far to find them (e.g. Briggs, 1972; Salmon, 1966, additionally, the 1982 Syllabus for Mental Health, the Mental Health Act 1982, and area, regional, district, and unit strategies for mental illness or health); mental health does not stand alone amid these changes, for they are found throughout the NHS. And yet our lasting impression is that, at the least, the management of these changes has been poor, and at worst, it has been disastrous.

This has led to the waste of precious resources, particularly in terms of the people involved, and the creation of an atmosphere in which any change is viewed with suspicion, if not hostility. We reluctantly draw attention to the Royal College of Nursing's (1985) controversial reaction to the Griffiths Report (1984) as an example of just such suspicion and hostility. In due course we shall be able to judge the response to the forthcoming White Paper on primary health care and be able to monitor the way in which the resultant changes are managed.

This concluding chapter proposes a model for change that is both efficient and effective as well as being demonstrably successful. We offer it to those working with change and those managing change, for we are concerned that change is not always managed well. We believe that health care is a dynamic concept and change is necessary to sustain it. In the past, perhaps, change has been a Catch-22 option, where the problems of badly managed change have been less attractive than maintaining a less than adequate status quo (large psychiatric hospitals being a case in point). With the increasing and justifiable involvement of people in health care, maintaining the status quo is no longer an option and therefore the focus must be in improving the ways in which we manage and facilitate change.

9.2 THE PURPOSE OF THIS BOOK

There will be readers perhaps who have managed to read and absorb this book in its entirety before coming to this last chapter and, we suspect, there will be others who come straight to this last chapter in the hope of finding all the answers. The book has been designed to work both ways. Here we present a summary and working model that can be applied in a variety of settings. The preceding chapters have offered readers the details, the pitfalls, and the justification — now the model can be taken in isolation. However, we caution that while this model is simple in the outline, it does require thought and skill in application. The fact that we have encompassed eight chapters on the details of facilitating change serves to illustrate its complex nature. For both types of reader we present a brief overview of the issues addressed in the book as an introduction to the model itself.

Summary

In this book we have been concerned with how health care workers go about the business of facilitating change, and we believe that through trial and error we have come up with a workable, indeed, the most effective way of facilitating change.

Throughout the book we have woven the threads of practical examples into the theoretical discussion, and all these have been drawn from mental health care. It is a most appropriate setting, for mental health is about involving people and about their relationships. Although other health care settings are about just these same issues, they are often obscured by technology, treatment, and curing. More important, mental health care has, along with caring for the elderly, been the Cinderella of the NHS. Under-resourced, it is consequently undertaken in a poor environment. If change can be achieved within these constraints, then it augurs well for using the model elsewhere.

Specifically the practical examples are drawn from nursing on the so-called psychogeriatric wards of a Victorian institution, which we have already described. Thus we have a setting that maximizes the obstacles to achieving change. We hope that these examples have helped bring down to earth the theoretical discussions and have interested readers. It does not matter if you are not familiar with the mental health setting or that you are not a nurse. What we have tried to show is how change affects people, and how they deal with it; no matter where you work with people, successful change involves those people. Each chapter in the book has its place in solving the puzzle of facilitating change.

Chapter 1

This chapter illustrates the perspective that is gained from taking a historical view of the setting. In our case, the setting is psychiatric nursing and its values, but a similar exercise could be done with other aspects of health care. What is significant here is the understanding that results from such a perspective: cause and effect are described and illustrated from 'classical' discussions in the literature; the effect on present-day thinking is sketched; and the development of a body of knowledge that represents the current state of the art is outlined. This perspective also flags up current key themes or changes that are facing participants. In our setting, the people involved, nurses and patients, are facing the transition from hospital to community and the move towards individualized care.

Chapter 2

Here we take the educational perspective and examine contemporary themes in education. Along with groupwork, research, and management, the educational perspective is a cornerstone of the model we propose for facilitating change. Again, we draw from our own setting, namely post-basic nurse education. But we argue strongly that the themes are similar whether you are a social worker, occupational therapist, physiotherapist, psychiatrist, or any other health care worker. Wherever change is taking place, the educationist is a key facilitator, and this chapter examines the teaching methods and learning styles of such a change agent. Throughout health care traditional practices are being challenged, and this chapter illustrates and discusses the basis for these challenges.

Chapter 3
Using the setting of the authors' work with managing change, this chapter concerns itself with the culture and issues within the specific change area. However, the importance of the chapter in the context of the whole book is in the range of issues it raises to do with change:

traditional approaches
staffing
blocks to learning
motivation
skill mix
components of change

While all these are of importance, the chapter focuses on motivation. Motivation is the key to a range of problems and warrants a good deal of attention. The discussion draws out the main aspects of motivation for the reader to consider but we acknowledge that the issue is complex. Our approach to change, we argue, increases motivation by valuing each individual's contribution.

Chapter 4
We move on in this chapter to an exploration of the second cornerstone of the work, namely groupwork. Drawing on our own project work, the chapter examines different types of groups and how they operate, illustrating the outcomes of groupwork and, in particular, the value they have for individuals participating in them. In challenging times in health care, not just in mental health nor just in the United Kingdom, we think the groupwork approach is of enormous importance because of the way in which it succeeds in facilitating change and winning people over to that change. We illustrate by reference to practical data, and define the structure and purpose of groups for all who are interested in groupwork.

Chapter 5

The third cornerstone of the work, research, is the focus of this chapter. In health care, people have modelled their research efforts on the natural sciences and medicine. It has not been until comparatively recently that we have considered the appropriateness of this course. Health care is multi-faceted and we have strongly argued that this should be reflected in our approach to research.

This chapter examines the decision-making process when it comes to research, arguing the advantages and disadvantages of different approaches; action research, as a research framework, is advocated for the work of facilitating change. The chapter, then, provides a reference-point for anyone faced with the choice of how to approach research, and the various methods are discussed with reference to the literature. It is interesting that the case for action research is argued by Hunt (1987) as a means of achieving or aiding the implementation of research findings. There appears to be a growing awareness of the need to look more flexibly at the way in which research is undertaken in health care.

Chapter 6

The purpose of this chapter is to present the evidence from the project of which we were a part, that our approach is successful in achieving change, and here the problem was not in scraping the barrel for any evidence of change, but rather to select from a large amount of data the most interesting examples of change. This chapter is specifically about our particular project in the management of change, and testament to all those involved in this work.

Chapter 7

The fourth and final cornerstone of the work, management, is the focus of this chapter. Structural considerations are of great importance when change is being considered and the type of structural support is discussed. Structural approaches are assessed and the methods we used in our project are illustrated. To help the reader understand the nature of the structural changes, the concept of change itself is examined, and the structural changes are then outlined within the various frameworks; as in other chapters, the text is illustrated by reference to our own work.

Chapter 8

It is a feature of all research work that, at its end, researchers are left with more questions than they originally set out to answer.

This chapter considers but a few of the issues that have arisen from our work of managing change, and are presented to enable the reader to have knowledge and forewarning of the material that working with change can produce. Each is important: values, ethics, ownership, culture, developing people, continuity, training and general management. In addition there were many other issues.

In this last chapter we make no grand claims for the model that we have been using during the past four years, save that it does work and, above all, it works for the people involved.

Foundations

The earlier chapters have cited two models of change which we used to construct our cornerstones: group work; research; education; and management. Our project design is based upon the frameworks provided by Lewin (1948) and Benne and Chinn (1985). Lewin's developmental systems approach is concerned with change within a system, while Benne and Chinn present more general strategies. Our model is the outcome of a lively process which was fuelled, styled and driven by the people who participated in it.

In a world where change is perpetual and rapid, there are two main perspectives which help the caring professions. One view sees man in a physical and biological manner and thus uses mechanical methods of enquiry to draw a picture of the world, while the other views man as basically a creature capable of love, caring and truth and thus uses subjective methods of enquiry to paint a very different picture of the world: we have not been happy with either of these diametrically opposed standpoints.

Our view is that people are potentially free when they choose, in as much as they are determined not only by physical and chemical properties, but may act as a sculptor to shape an change the environment. He responds to others and acts upon them. He is not merely the product of his own history but plays a significant part in his future. In short, people grow and change.

Our model therefore combines philosophy, a view of the world, with a way of working which draws upon past models of change. Not unlike man our prototype model is fuelled from within and each example of this model in use will develop a unique structure, process and outcome. However the model we now present will always rise from the same foundation cornerstones using the specific principles forged during the Management of Change Project.

9.3 MODEL FOR CHANGE

Our intention in describing a model is that health care workers can take the framework and use it in their own settings to facilitate change.

The model is dynamic, it moves and progresses. This allows each separate movement to be seen and described. It also allows it to generate different outcomes. Essentially the model is a multifired engine. Within the engine the fuels are converted using a catalyst into energy which drives three interlocking wheels. The wheels form an infinitely variable pattern as they interlock. A diagrammatic representation of this is presented in Fig. 9.1, together with some of the patterns possible in Fig. 9.2. While this may look intriguing, the purpose is serious. Our engine is driving change, and each of the wheels is a component of the model of change.

Wheel A = structural set-up;
Wheel B = operational process;
Wheel C = outcome questions.

Each wheel interlocks to differing degrees by the energy generated by the converter.

As with most engines, the drive is governed by gears which are externally selected and engaged as, for example, when a senior manager slows things down or tries to quicken the pace of change.

The fuel is, of course, people – and we will discuss the right ingredients of the best fuel! Our energy converter is action research, and the catalyst is groupwork (educators). The energy converter uses fuel (people) to drive the wheels (change). So the model of change can be viewed as an engine whose product is change as illustrated in Fig. 9.3. If we look inside the engine we can see what makes it work.

Fuel

No dynamic machine or model runs without fuel and, in our model, the fuel is people. As with all fuels, the right combination of

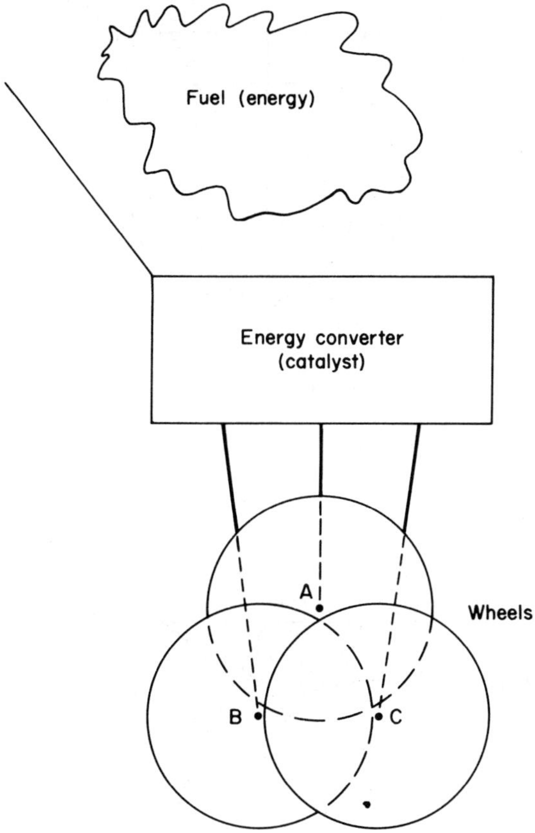

Fig. 9.1 A diagrammatic engine.

constituents is essential. To a certain extent, the change agents (group facilitators at the chalkface and the steering group at the project operational level) engaged the interlocking wheels and set the gear. This is an interesting example of the dynamics of the model. For instance, within the Ward Team Staff Support Groups you have three facilitators conducting the five groups. The facilitators themselves are supervised by the project team. The facilitators have a support group to monitor their own development and change as individuals, while the project team co-ordinates structural changes with the hospital managers, e.g. duty rota changes that enable the ten ward sisters to work every Thursday. Therefore, the

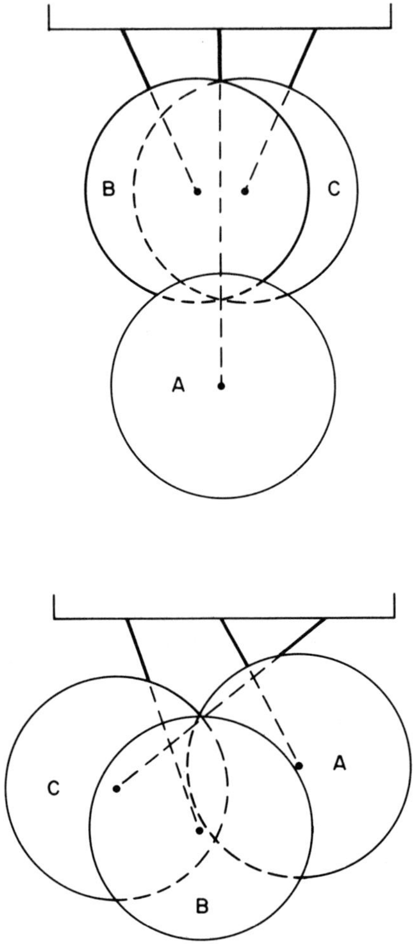

Fig. 9.2 Examples of different configurations.

instrument of regulation between the engine and wheels is the dynamic action within itself of the catalyst, the change agent. The catalyst/change agent allows the engine to maximize the use of the fuel/people. The change agent is involved in designing the best possible type of engine and ensuring that it runs to its full potential by acting as a catalyst, i.e. monitoring, evaluating, changing, acting, and facilitating.

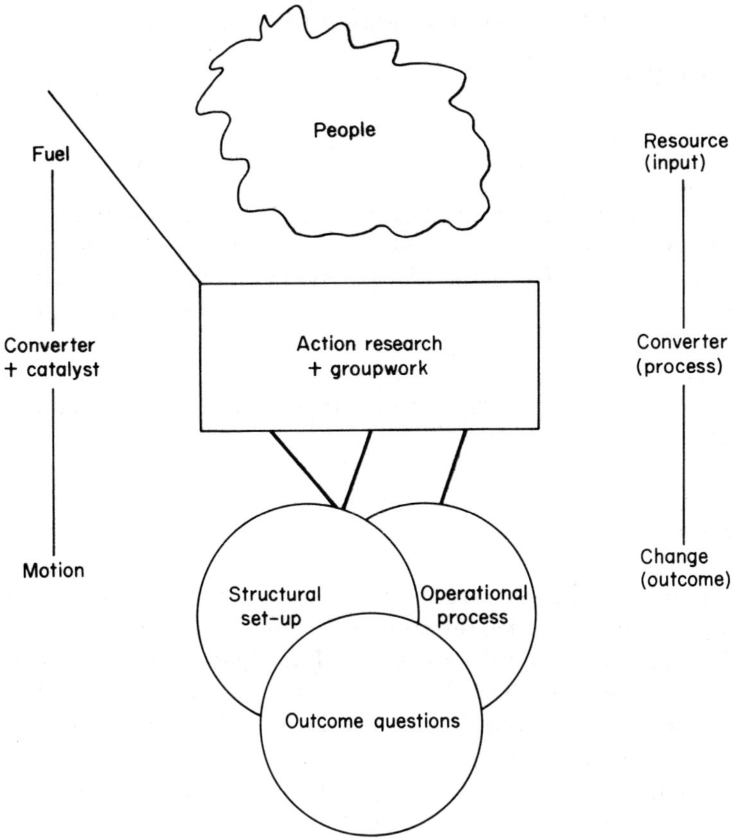

Fig. 9.3 The model of change.

The point about the interlocking of the wheels is that we are saying that human beings are very much in the driving seat of our model. Thus the construction of the model will be very different each time it is used, whether in the same or in differing settings. The interworkings of our model allow for human goodness and badness to be expressed and observed. The self-monitoring inherent in groupwork and individual growth (which we think is a part of learning nursing) means that at the heart of our model lies the notion and opportunity for personal change and skill development. That is the life blood, the fuel that drives our model/engine.

In our model the other key constituents that make up the fuel are:

managers
educators
researchers
practitioners/clients

The practitioners, our clients, are here the most important. The more practitioners involved, the richer the fuel. We also believe the fuel can be enriched by the addition of another ingredient, namely patients/clients/consumers. However, in the NHS the use of such a group/ingredient is only in its infancy.

The illustration serves us well because fuel of itself is often inert until it has been energized. In the NHS there is a lot of unutilized fuel!

Energy converter

To bring the fuel to life requires a catalyst. In the model we propose, the catalyst is groupwork in its broadest sense, and in which people are allowed to change. Experiential learning changes people. However, the role of the change agent as a part of the catalyst is equally important. Within a well-facilitated group a person feels valued and gives of their best. Of itself, fuel converted to energy is usually wasted and valueless, thus it needs to be channelled. The energy converter of our model uses action research to channel the energy produced; thus the cycles of action research are likened to a series of combustion cycles. Again, it is perhaps worth taking our illustration one step further. We like to view our fuel as nuclear in nature, as it is self-regenerating and contagious! Consequently, like all nuclear fuel, it needs to be handled carefully. Individual constituents of the fuel, individual people, are easily 'burnt out', and it is only together that they are long-lasting.

Working of the converter

The converter works by using a cycle of action research which can be run as many times as is necessary or as it is resourced. In diagrammatic form what is happening is a spiral of such action cycles (Fig. 9.4). Each time a cycle takes place, the pattern of

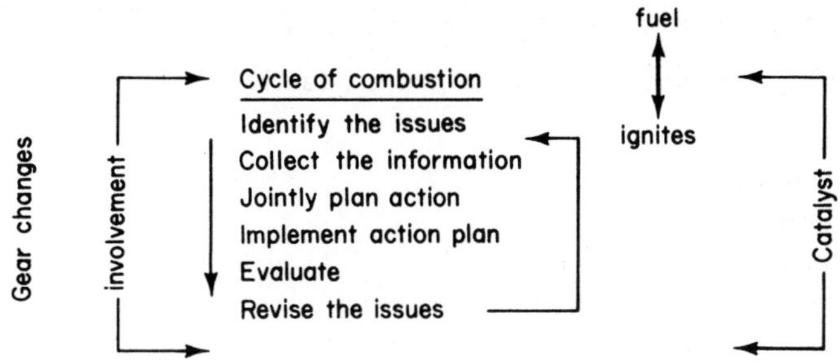

Fig. 9.4 Cycle of action research.

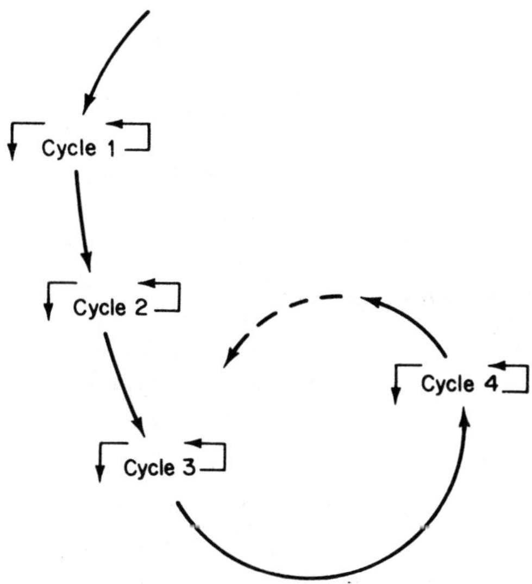

Fig. 9.5 Cycles of energy.

interlocking wheels changes, representing changes occurring in structure, process, or outcome, or a mixture of two or three (Fig. 9.5).

Wheels

If we look in detail at each of these wheels, we can see that they have many component pieces.

Wheel A: structural set-up

Parts Organization of resources people, funds.

time
setting
environment
targets
politics
administration (forms, policies, etc.)
records

Wheel B: operational processes

Parts	
values	difficulties
rules	interference
culture	teaching
permission	learning
methods	group dynamics
measures	dependence

Wheel C: outcome questions

Parts	
need	care outcomes
desired values	staff development
objectives	competencies
relationships	

As has been described, the wheels interlock and at different times they assume different relationships. Thus, in running the engine, the operational processes influence structure and the outcome and vice versa.

It is also worth noting that until the engine starts to run the outcomes are in terms of questions. As the engine gets going these outcome questions become linked with outcome answers.

Building the engine

As within any institution, there are component parts of the engine to assemble in this model for change. In the setting of the project we undertook, we assembled the model from the bits that we found, often lying around unused! The job of building the model for change can fall to any of the individuals within the institution, or it is imported by change agents. The constructor of our project was Bill Lemmer; and backing him up were a team of enthusiastic builders, who helped lay the cornerstones and support and guide the project structure as it was given life by the five ward teams collaborating with the Steering Group.

Running the engine

Once constructed, according to the blueprints presented in the preceding chapters, the model is guaranteed to run well. However, as with all constructions, it needs regular attention to ensure smooth running, and here is the key role of the facilitator/researcher/educator. The constituents of the fuel, the people, need to be involved in the right collaborative framework. The catalyst needs to be supported and the facilitator needs to control the groups. The energy converter needs to be switched on and monitored. All are time-consuming processes, but they are essential if the model for change is to run smoothly.

Motion

The result of the model is change, the wheels move round. Although the pattern of their interlocking is not predictable, as we have illustrated in the book, the general direction *is* controllable. Control is ensured through the skills of the facilitator, and these, in turn, involve people and their use, the process of converting them and the use of groupwork in the catalyst.

Masterplan

Using the chapters within this book as a reference, here is an outline plan for facilitating change:

Part of Model	*Action*
Wheels	Identify the need Clarify the values Set objectives and time Find resources
Construction	Collaboration – managers educationists researchers practitioners Design framework
Fuel	Get everyone together
Catalyst	Facilitator(s) Set up and run groups using:
Converter	Action research cycles issue information action evaluation
Wheels	Structural set-up Organizational process Outcome question and answers
AND REPEAT	

9.4 CONCLUSION

We have explored many issues in this book and drawn them together here to produce a post-basic educational model for change.

We know that this model works. We have demonstrated it in practice in one of the most difficult settings in health care, the institutionalized long-stay elderly mentally ill. We hope that we have demonstrated that it works to readers and, at the least, that some elements of the project will have a direct bearing on their own work and provide pointers for its future development.

We do not presume to suggest that this is the only way of facilitating change; however, we would suggest that, in our experience of health care, it is the best we have come across. We think it is valuable because it values all the individuals involved in an area, it maximizes available resources, and achieves a quality of change that is to be admired.

In the final analysis, then, we have given the bones of a new model that we have devised and developed. Each chapter in the book offers examples and perspectives hewn from the action and change of nursing today. We would predict, on the basis of our evidence, that the reader will find such an exercise richly rewarding.

REFERENCES

Benne, K.D. and Chinn, R. (1985) *The Planning of Change*, Holt, Rinehart and Winston, Eastbourne.

Briggs, A. (Chairman) (1972) *Report of the Committee on Nursing*, HMSO, London; October.

Griffiths, R. (Chairman) (1984) *NHS Management Inquiry*, HMSO, London.

Hunt, M. (1987) The process of translating research findings into nursing practice. *Journal of Advanced Nursing*, **12**, 101–10.

Lewin, K. (1948) *Resolving Social Conflicts*, Harper and Row, New York.

Salmon, B. (Chairman) (1966) *Report of the Committee on Senior Nursing Staff*, HMSO, London.

Index